D1266843

Northwestern University
STUDIES IN *Phenomenology &*
Existential Philosophy

GENERAL EDITOR
John Wild

ASSOCIATE EDITOR
James M. Edie

CONSULTING EDITORS
Hubert L. Dreyfus
William Earle
J. N. Findlay
Dagfinn Føllesdal
Marjorie Grene
Aron Gurwitsch
Emmanuel Levinas
Alphonso Lingis
Maurice Natanson
Paul Ricoeur
George Schrader
Calvin O. Schrag
Herbert Spiegelberg
Charles Taylor

McCORMICK THEOLOGICAL SEMINARY
McGAW MEMORIAL LIBRARY
800 WEST BELDEN AVENUE
CHICAGO, ILLINOIS 60614

The Theory of Intuition
in Husserl's
Phenomenology

Emmanuel Levinas

Translated by

The Theory of Intuition in Husserl's Phenomenology

ANDRÉ ORIANNE

NORTHWESTERN UNIVERSITY PRESS

EVANSTON   1973

Copyright © 1973 by Northwestern University Press
All rights reserved
Library of Congress Catalog Card Number: 72–96698
ISBN 0–8101–0413–X
Printed in the United States of America

Published in French under the title *Théorie de l'intuition
dans la phénoménologie de Husserl,* 1963, by Librairie
Philosophique J. Vrin.

André Orianne is Assistant Professor of Philosophy at The
Pennsylvania State University and Honorary *Aspirant* of
the Belgian FNRS (national fund for scientific research).

Contents

1-27-74
Deg

B
3279
. H94
L46
1973

Translator's Foreword

Because of the particular nature of Levinas' book, I feel that I should explain briefly why the publication of this translation is not only a worthwhile but a necessary task.

The Theory of Intuition [1] was written over forty years ago, when only a fragment of Husserl's thought was available to commentators. Undeniably, Husserlian scholarship has grown immensely since its publication. Even Levinas considers it somewhat outdated now. Yet I believe that it is of far more than merely historical interest.

Whatever progress has been made in Husserlian scholarship, *The Theory of Intuition* still remains the best commentary we have on Husserl's most central work, *Ideen I*. This alone would justify our translation. But there is more. Emmanuel Levinas is in his own right an important philosopher, and for that reason none of his works should leave us indifferent. Even when he writes on Husserl and modestly puts himself in the background to let Husserl's thought unfold itself, Levinas is too much of a philosopher to be a mere "historian." As he says himself, it is to a living thought and not to a closed system that he wants to introduce us. [2] In this living thought Levinas himself is engaged. Husserl was one of the major influences on Levinas' own philoso-

---

1. Emmanuel Levinas, *Théorie de l'intuition dans la phénoménologie de Husserl* (Paris: Alcan, 1930; Vrin, 1963) (subsequently abbreviated as *TI* below).
2. *TI*, p. xxxiii.

[xi]

phy. Thus Levinas' first attempt to confront Husserl's thought was also his first attempt to confront his own thought.

As will be made clear in my closing historical remarks, this work is dated. That is why I have concentrated here on the development of Levinas' reflection on Husserl as it occurred between 1930 and 1965. This development has been influenced both by the growing availability of Husserl's writings and by Levinas' own philosophical evolution. Hence I hope that, by taking these factors into account, I may here contribute to the "updating" of *The Theory of Intuition*—which, despite its limitations, remains, I believe, of lasting importance.

LEVINAS' REFLECTION ON HUSSERL AND ITS DEVELOPMENT

IN PRESENTING THESE BRIEF NOTES, I have concentrated on two main themes in Levinas' writings on Husserl, the problem of the metaphysical foundation of the reduction and the problem of sensation, since I think that they best reflect Levinas' changing relationship to Husserl's thought. They are also crucial problems for a serious understanding of Husserlian phenomenology.

In the conclusions of *Theory of Intuition*, Levinas reproaches Husserl for not having questioned the possibility and the foundation of the transcendental reduction.[3] However, Husserl does raise this question toward the beginning of *Ideen* (§ 31), when he explains the possibility of the reduction by appealing to the Cartesian doubt. The Cartesian doubt (and, apparently, the reduction itself) is based on our freedom to deny any theoretical judgment. This freedom is restricted to the level of theory[4] and does not engage the total life of the *Homo philosophus*.[5]

Thus, there is a very close connection between the way the reduction is presented in *Ideen* and the thesis of the primacy of theoretical consciousness, one of Levinas' main targets of criticism in *Theory of Intuition*. This connection can be better under-

3. *Ibid.*, p. 157.
4. *Ibid.*
5. *Ibid.*, pp. 155–56. See also Ricoeur's commentary in his French translation of *Ideen*: "The freedom in question here cannot yet be understood" (E. Husserl, *Idées directrices pour une phénoménologie*, trans. P. Ricoeur [Paris: Gallimard, 1950], p. 99, n. 1).

stood in reference to one of the central theses of *Ideen:* the absoluteness of consciousness.

The absoluteness of consciousness

One of Levinas' major theses in *Theory of Intuition* is that phenomenology transcends its apparently epistemological starting point to develop into a full-fledged ontology. The reduction, as opposed to the Cartesian doubt, is not a temporary measure of prudence but the necessary and permanent opening of a true ontological realm. This thesis can be substantiated only by a careful analysis of the absoluteness of consciousness.

Since anything's mode of being is its way of being experienced, the characteristic mode of existing of consciousness is that, in reflection, consciousness is not given through *Abschattungen*—or, as Levinas puts it, there is no duality between what is intimated and what is present.[6] In Husserl's terms, this means that there is no duality between being and appearance.[7] That which is given in reflection is given absolutely in the sense of not being dependent on further experiences for its confirmation. Adequation, and thereby certainty (since uncertainty is bound to the fact that transcendent objects are never given in their totality), characterize the perception of consciousness. From this it follows that consciousness necessarily exists, in the sense that it is impossible to deny its existence. This is the Cartesian thesis. But Husserl's intentions go considerably further than Descartes's. Descartes remains at a purely epistemological level, satisfied with the *certainty* that consciousness exists, that I doubt, think, etc. However, for Husserl, it is not only our *knowledge* of the existence of consciousness and of its *Erlebnisse* which is absolute, but that existence itself. Furthermore, Husserl wants to reverse the order of the Cartesian terms. Even though the absoluteness of consciousness is revealed through the adequation of its perception, for Husserl it is the absoluteness of consciousness which *founds* adequate perception. As Levinas says, "The absolute evidence of the *cogito* is founded on the mode of being of consciousness."[8]

6. *TI,* p. 26–27.
7. *Ideen,* § 42, p. 77.
8. *TI,* p. 28.

Conscious life exists prior to reflection inasmuch as what is perceived in reflection is always given as having already been there.[9] This is also true of transcendent perception in that whatever appears does so as being already part of a previous horizon. But the essential difference between the two cases is that my perceptual horizon is not infinite. The whole perceptual world does not belong by right to my horizon as does the world of my *Erlebnisse* which, "through their very manner of existing," [10] always fulfill the conditions necessary to be reflected upon.

The absoluteness of consciousness is understood here in a purely theoretical sense. It is the readiness of *Erlebnisse* to be perceived, and perception is a theoretical act. This account is unsatisfactory inasmuch as this readiness itself cannot be justified while remaining on merely theoretical ground.

The thesis of the absoluteness of consciousness is central to the two problems we shall examine. I have already sketched its relevance to the problem of the reduction. It is equally important with respect to the problem of sensation, which we shall examine below. Sensation can be viewed as a challenge to the absoluteness of consciousness, inasmuch as it introduces within consciousness an irreducible element of passivity.[11]

More generally, phenomenology requires us to understand how consciousness can at the same time be absolute and intentional, that is, open (or relative) to anything genuinely other than itself.

In the following pages, we shall try to show how Levinas solves those problems by reinterpreting the significance of theoretical life and thereby providing a better understanding and a firmer foundation for the absoluteness of consciousness.

The transcendental reduction as the freedom of consciousness

In 1940, Levinas published a paper on "L'Oeuvre d'Edmond Husserl." [12] Despite a basic continuity between his interpretation

---

9. *Ideen*, § 45, p. 83.

10. *Ibid.*, p. 84.

11. See E. Levinas, "Intentionalité et sensation," *Revue internationale de philosophie*, XIX (1965), 38 (subsequently abbreviated as *IS*).

12. Reprinted in and quoted from *En découvrant l'existence avec Husserl et Heidegger* (Paris: Vrin, 1949) (subsequently abbreviated as *OEH*).

of Husserl there and in *Theory of Intuition,* there are two striking differences. One is the prominence given in "L'Oeuvre" to the
concept of freedom; the other is the related attempt to reevaluate
the significance of Husserl's "intellectualism." [13]

To introduce these new developments, we must first return
to the notion of intentionality, the essence of consciousness.
"Intentionality is essentially an act of *Sinngebung.*" [14] The reduction reveals this constitutive character of intentionality: "The
world that has to be conquered after the phenomenological reduction is a world *constituted* by a thought." [15] It follows that evidence (the totally fulfilled intentional act) must be called free,[16]
since an object is revealed only inasmuch as it is understood
(i.e., *given* a sense or constituted). This is crucial for understanding the absoluteness of consciousness, because absolute
evidence is but the epistemological aspect of the absoluteness
of consciousness.

"Consciousness is not relative to anything because it is
free." [17] The reversal of the Cartesian terms in *Theory of Intuition* takes a new form here. "The total possession of oneself
in reflection is but the other [epistemological] side of freedom." [18]

This understanding of the absoluteness of consciousness as
freedom gives us a new perspective on the reduction. "The reduction," says Levinas, "is a manner for the mind . . . to be free." [19]
"The phenomenological reduction is an act of violence that man
does to himself . . . in order to find himself again as pure
thought." [20]

This new insight into the nature of the reduction and the
meaning of the absoluteness of consciousness depends, in the
last analysis, on a reinterpretation of intentionality as liberation
from the world rather than (or, at least, as well as) presence to
the world.

We must next show how these new insights lead Levinas to
modify his attitude toward Husserl's "intellectualism."

13. In fact, Levinas proposes to abandon this epithet (*OEH,* p.
23).
    14. *Ibid.,* p. 11.
    15. *Ibid.,* p. 38; italics added.
    16. *Ibid.*
    17. *Ibid.*
    18. *Ibid.*
    19. *Ibid.*
    20. *Ibid.,* p. 36. As we shall see, *pure thought* must not be under-
stood as pure *theoretical* thought.

In the conclusion of *Theory of Intuition,* Levinas opposes Husserl's theory of intuition to that of Bergson. For Bergson, he says, philosophical intuition is ultimately an act of freedom. It thus has a metaphysical foundation which it lacks in Husserl.[21] For Husserl, "Philosophy begins with the reduction. This is an act in which we consider life . . . but no longer live it." [22] In the metaphysical order, the concrete living individual is object before being subject.

We have shown the difference between this conclusion and those of "L'Oeuvre." We must now determine how the progress made in "L'Oeuvre" follows from a reinterpretation of the thesis of the primacy of theory. This thesis was defined in *Theory of Intuition* as the fact that a representation (*Vorstellung*) is at the basis of all acts of consciousness. We must therefore return to the function of representation in Husserl's philosophy, and to its interpretation by Levinas, in order to grasp fully Levinas' new attitude toward Husserl's intellectualism.

"L'Oeuvre" reasserts, with as much vigor as *Theory of Intuition,* the primacy of theoretical consciousness. But the crucial difference between the two is that in "L'Oeuvre" Levinas presents objectification and representation as logically contained in the idea of sense. This is intimated when Levinas says: "It would probably be unjust to call [Husserl's philosophy] intellectualist. The primacy given to the notion of sense with respect to that of object in characterizing thought forbids it." [23] Nevertheless, "The object constitutes a necessary moment of the very phenomenon of sense." [24] This is what the idea of intentionality implies.

Intentionality, understood as *Sinngebung,* consists in the synthesis of an ideal identity through the multiplicity of conscious *Erlebnisse.* All intentional thought therefore involves us in a process of identification, that is, of objectification. This act of objectification, or of synthesis, is precisely what Husserl understands by representation. In this sense, representation is not opposed to feeling and desire but is an integral part of them. All intentionality is representative inasmuch as its object is determined by a sense (i.e., an identifying synthesis) but not by being at bottom "contemplative" (theoretical). In other words, the ob-

21. *TI,* p. 146.
22. *Ibid.*
23. *OEH,* p. 23.
24. *Ibid.,* p. 22.

jectifying (representative) act which is presupposed by all acts of consciousness need not be a theoretical act. Any signifying act is objectifying. That which is wanted or desired is not an object of contemplation, it is not a thing.[25] These assertions in "L'Oeuvre" differ sharply from what Levinas says in *Theory of Intuition:* "Even if the objects of complex acts, such as will, desire, etc., exist in another manner than do the objects of simple representation, they still must have to some extent the mode of existence of theoretical objects." [26]

But, in "L'Oeuvre," the primacy of theoretical consciousness is not only reinterpreted, it is also (positively) reevaluated. Levinas asks, "What does the presence of an act of identification [representation] mean as the basis of intentions that are in no way intellectual?" [27] The key to the answer is the notion of evidence. "Every intention is a search for evidence." [28] Evidence is found through the process of identification, that is, through representation. Evidence is the key to understanding the value of representation in consciousness. Evidence, for Husserl, is not a feeling. It is the very relation between subject and object, not as mere presence (brute fact) but as understanding. It is the fulfillment of intentionality as *Sinngebung,* and the act of *Sinngebung* is the act which realizes the freedom of consciousness.

The primacy of theory, as it has been reinterpreted here, appears finally as the condition for a consciousness whose freedom is not purely negative (random or arbitrary). The freedom of the *Sinngebung* would be empty if it did not meet, in evidence, a world which is given as well as constituted. "The evidence of a world which is given . . . is the *positive* realization of freedom." [29] Evidence is that without which consciousness would not be the origin of being. If there is to be origin of being, there must be being. Being is given in evidence, and evidence presupposes representation.

Hence, ultimately it is the understanding of intentionality as *Sinngebung* (i.e., as freedom oriented toward or motivated by a sense) which allows Levinas to answer two of the crucial questions in *Theory of Intuition,* that of the "existential" meaning of the reduction and that of the primacy of theory. The answer to

25. *Ibid.,* p. 24.
26. *TI,* p. 62.
27. *OEH,* p. 24.
28. *Ibid.*
29. *Ibid.;* italics added.

the first question is that the reduction is the exercise of the existential freedom of consciousness as it becomes fully aware of itself. The second question is answered by the recognition that only a theoretical (in the sense of objectifying) consciousness can be free without being empty and losing itself into nothingness.

Intentionality and sensation

To a large extent, *Theory of Intuition* fails to recognize the problematic aspect of the relationship between intentionality and sensation. Levinas' primary concern is to emphasize the radical difference between Husserl's transcendental idealism and the sensationalist idealism of a Berkeley. For this, it is necessary and sufficient to emphasize Husserl's theory of the intentionality of sensations. There is, for Husserl, a radical distinction between the act of sensation and its intentional object, a sensible quality. A sensation is a specific intentional mode of animation of hyletic data in which they are taken as "analogous" to sensible qualities.[30]

This approach to sensation, which goes back to *LU*, contains a number of problems, not the least of which is the tension within Husserl's own thought between idealism (animation) and sensualism (analogy). Neither of these two crucial terms (animation and analogy) is seriously investigated in *Theory of Intuition*.

Both *Theory of Intuition* and "L'Oeuvre" strongly emphasize the idea of animation. In "L'Oeuvre," particularly, Levinas comes close to viewing sensations as mere abstracts of more complex intentional acts: "The contents of consciousness are not merely animated by a meaning but *are* meanings. They are therefore *inseparable* from the essences they mean. . . . Consciousness and its real contents do not 'weight' as reality but remain [pure] meaning through intentionality."[31]

This interpretation is tempting inasmuch as it restores the absolute intentionality of consciousness in all its transparence.

30. As we shall see, the relation between hyletic data and intentionality runs even deeper, since the hyletic level is itself constituted through a special mode of intentionality which forms the basis of the consciousness of immanent time.

31. *OEH*, p. 31; italics added.

Unfortunately, it seems impossible to reconcile it with Husserl's theory of the constitution of the hyletic level. Moreover, it makes the whole notion of analogy even more difficult, if not impossible, to understand. Hence it seems necessary to go beyond *Theory of Intuition* and analyze that level of intentionality at which hyletic data (and their senses) are constituted. This leads us to consider the problem of temporality.[32]

In one sense, the present is, for Husserl, the "now-point." Everything begins with the *Urimpression,* and *here* we seem to have a genuine abstraction, something like a "brute fact." It is an ultimate unintelligible, itself nonconstituted, from which all constitution originates. At the same time and for the same reason it is never "given," and in that sense it does not exist. Yet, for Husserl, the *genuine* present is not a mere point but has duration; it is protention and retention. An *Urimpression* is never given outside this horizon. It is always caught in a structure of impressions which are present only on the mode of "has just been" or "is about to be." The "now-point" is at once absolute (but also abstract, empty) freedom and absolute passivity. This is where "it all begins," but this is also where consciousness never is and has neither being nor freedom. The present has always already lost its "presence" (in the sense of brute facticity), because it has fallen in the retention of the past which is a form of intentionality.

This is how we must understand the crucial notion of *animation.* Animation is not the injection of a sense into a senseless datum. It is the act in which at once the datum and the sense appear as present in the form of protention or retention.

In 1964, Levinas returns to the problem of sensation in his paper "Intentionalité et sensation." There we find not only a deeper reflection on the concepts of freedom, temporality, and evidence but also a new recognition of the importance of the place of the body within conscious life.

In "L'Oeuvre" the problem of sensation was tentatively solved at the expense of leaving aside the analogical character of sensations. But this character cannot be ignored, since it is essential to Husserl's theory of evidence. In order to examine the relationship between sensation and evidence we must return to *LU* and the notion of *Fülle.*

32. *Ibid.,* pp. 41 ff.

Husserl certainly never confused sensation and evidence. He never identified our sensations with the sensible qualities they represent. But it is precisely this idea of representation that Levinas seriously questions in "Intentionalité." In *LU*, sensations are characterized as resembling or analogous to (although different from) the sensible qualities of objects. In *Ideen*, sensations are the *Abschattungen* through which these qualities are constituted. But the very notion of resemblance, Levinas points out, presupposes the constitution of an objective sphere. This notion thereby threatens the radical distinction (so strongly asserted and so essential for Husserl) between sensations and sensible qualities. We find the threat of sensualistic empiricism lurking again in the background. This threat is reinforced by the notion of *Fülle*, according to which the function of sensation seems precisely to insure the intuitive fullness of the object.

Husserl characterized intuitive, as opposed to merely symbolic, acts by reference to intentionality. In an intuitive act, consciousness *"claims"* to hold its object "in flesh and blood." It would have been sheer naïveté to expect to be able to reduce the distinction between symbolic and intuitive thought (that is, ultimately, to reduce evidence) to a mere "claim" of consciousness. Hence the theory of fullness. But what neither Husserl (at least in *LU* and in *Ideen I*) nor Levinas (so far) had realized were the difficulties involved in understanding the relationships between those two components of intuition. Levinas expresses the situation in the clearest possible terms when he says "an intuitive act is at once an intention of presence and the indispensable presence of a content in a subject." [33] If both elements are necessary, we seem to be driven to a Kantian model where the function of the understanding is to give form to a sensible content. Yet such a Kantian interpretation of Husserl is ruled out by the general intention of his philosophy.

The first approach to a solution of this problem in "Intentionalité" is similar to that adopted in "L'Oeuvre." We must return to the *Urimpression* and, by way of temporality, gain a better understanding of intentionality and sensation together rather than in opposition to each other. Sensation is not a mere coincidence between sensing and what is being sensed. Between the two there is a "minimal distance" in time which is called

33. *IS*, p. 40.

intentionality. If, as Derrida claims,[34] Husserl's philosophy is a metaphysics of presence, the presence must always be understood as modification. There is coincidence between intention and event, but this coincidence takes the form of a "no longer there" or a "not yet there" without which there could not be "presence-for." We shall later discuss this dialectic of presence and distance (temporality), since it involves some of the crucial aspects of Husserlian phenomenology.

As we have observed, one of the novelties of "Intentionalité" is the importance it gives to the function of the body. Husserl's and Levinas' concern to mark the radical difference between phenomenology and sensualistic empiricism had led them to give a primarily negative analysis of the role of the body. However, once all naturalistic (causal) interpretation of sensation has been unambiguously set aside, there remains room for a more positive approach to the place of the body within the problem of sensation. Sensation is the locus of an essential passivity in consciousness, a passivity which we have grown to recognize as a precondition rather than an antithesis to the freedom of intentionality. This passivity indicates a certain way for consciousness of being in the world. Levinas wants us to see now that "the corporeity of consciousness is the exact measure of this participation of consciousness to the world constituted by it." [35] The experience of sensation is also the experience of corporeity. Things are felt "at the tips of our fingers." In *Ideen II*, Husserl calls this feeling *Empfindnis*. It is an experience which overcomes the duality of the sentient and the sensed, the subject and the object. The feeling of my pen in my hand defies this duality. In it, the feeling of the pen and the felt pen (as such) are indistinguishable.

An *Empfindnis* is more than just localized in space; it is the experience of space itself. This is the characteristic experience of the hyletic level and constitutes the spatiality of consciousness. It is absurd to say, of a fully intentional *Erlebnis*, that it has a place (in my head, for example). But this feeling of pain I have is (and it is a matter of eidetic necessity) in my left or my right foot. My *Empfindnisse* not only locate me in space but they reveal

34. Jacques Derrida, *La Voix et le phénomène* (Paris: Presses Universitaires de France, 1967), English translation by David B. Allison, *Speech and Phenomena* (Evanston, Ill.: Northwestern University Press, 1973).

35. *IS,* p. 48.

me as incarnated, as spatial consciousness. I can feel heat in my hand and hardness under my foot. I am extended.

The notion of *Empfindnis* eliminates the duality between sensation and sensible qualities without reducing either to the other. An *Empfindnis* itself is neither a sensation nor a quality but the foundation of both. This common foundation, rooted in the corporeity of consciousness, throws an important light on the notion of analogy.

But one can go further. My body is not only the spatialization of my consciousness but also its mobility. This essential mobility of consciousness is implied (yet unexpressed) in the whole theory of perception by *Abschattungen*. Husserl did not develop this idea until *Ideen II*. It is the idea of mobility which will help make sense of the notion of analogy when it is applied to full-fledged sensations in their function of *Fülle*.

The analogy between sensible qualities and sensations is not (as it would appear to a naïve but straightforward interpretation) a reflection or a mirroring of one in the other as in empiricism. Rather, it is the *constitution* of one by the other. That a statue, for example, is always given in *Abschattungen* means that I can *move* around it, tilt, lower, or raise my head, and that through each of those *movements* the object will be given in a different viewpoint. To say that there is an analogy between the sensible qualities and the sensations is not to say that the various sensible qualities of objects are "reflected" in my consciousness but that they are constituted through my freely moving around and adopting new viewpoints.

To summarize, the idea of *Empfindnis* carries the burden of explaining a notion of analogy that does not presuppose a pre-constituted objective realm. The idea of mobility helps us to understand the process of active constitution (intentional objectification). In turn, both the notion of *Empfindnis* and that of mobility express the corporeity of consciousness.

In conclusion, I would like to return to what I have called "the dialectic of presence and distance." This theme is totally absent from *Theory of Intuition*. It appears first in "L'Oeuvre" but is not developed until "Intentionalité."

In "L'Oeuvre" we find a first intimation that the distinction between immanence and transcendence may be the same as that between presence and nonpresence.[36] Only the immanent is pres-

36. *OEH*, p. 47.

ent in its totality and hence subject to adequate evidence. The transcendent is precisely such, not as the external opposed to the internal, but as what contains in itself an essential reference to an indefinite future (or past). Similar assertions can be found in "Intentionalité," where this theme is developed with much greater depth and vigor.[37]

We have seen that immanent intentionality was dependent on immanent time, that it was protention and retention. This applies to transcendent intentionality (such as perception) as well. To become perception, a sensation must be animated by a new intentionality, which again presupposes a "minimal distance" in time. But Levinas is mistaken when he sees here a remnant of the empiricist scheme. The temporal priority of sensations over perception does not suggest that sensations function as "building blocks," as they do in empiricism. On the contrary, we know that the whole object is given in any *Abschattung*. But it is given as intentional, and all intentional objects as such are ideal. In one sense only can we say that perceived objects are constructed from sensations. They are constructed in time in the sense of being intended, constituted as ideal objects, as what remains permanent in time. Hence time is essential to both immanent and transcendent intentionality. There can never be perfect coincidence between an act and its object. Concepts such as evidence or adequation must be understood in the light of this primary noncoincidence.

In perception, however, temporality takes on a further dimension. In "Intentionalité" Levinas asks: "Is all transcendent intentionality already in some way memory?"[38] Levinas does not answer. But the problem of memory must ultimately be raised if we want to reach the level of truly objectifying intentionality. We have said that there is no intentionality without representation, that is, without *Vorstellung*. But representation also means *Vergegenwärtigung* (re-presentation), re-presentation which goes beyond the immanent present. Husserl has given us the means to understand the meaning of temporality, the essential repetitive structure (ideality) involved in consciousness within the sphere of the immanent present (including protentions and retentions). However, there is another aspect of temporality which is no less essential to his philosophy: "that every act can

37. *IS*, p. 44.
38. *Ibid.*, p. 45.

be reproduced . . . in recollection, for example." [39] For Husserl, this remains a mere assertion. To develop it further would involve him in recognizing this essential historicity of consciousness which, in Levinas' words, means "that man has a specific manner of being his past." [40] Without recognizing this essential historicity, Husserl can never reach a level of fully objective (and intersubjective) intentionality. Let us be clear. Far from denying it, Husserl asserts the historicity of consciousness, as he asserts the existence of alter egos, and he even attempts to explain it. Yet there always seems to remain for him the *possibility* of a self-sufficient egological, ahistorical sphere of consciousness. It is here that Husserlian phenomenology is fundamentally irreconcilable with the philosophies of Heidegger or Merleau-Ponty. Yet this historical dimension becomes inescapable when, in Husserl's own terms, we understand consciousness as idealizing intentionality, as *Sinngebung*.

HISTORICAL REMARKS

IF THE READER is to understand fully the scope and meaning of this book, we must add here some (very sketchy) indications about the philosophical situation in France at the time of its publication.

In the late twenties two philosophies had virtual monopoly of the French philosophical academic scene: the intuitionism of Bergson and the rationalism of Brunschvicg. It is hardly exaggerating to say that the only thing they held in common was their rejection of the late-nineteenth-century Comtian positivism. This, at the same time, was their main source of attraction.[41] Yet neither of these philosophies (especially that of Brunschvicg and his fellow rationalists) seemed able to fulfill the needs of the younger generation of philosophers, influenced by such writers as Proust and Gide and scarred by the still fresh memories of World War I.[42] Brunschvicg's idealism seemed, both philosophi-

39. *Zeitbewusstsein*, Appendix XII.
40. *TI*, p. 156.
41. This is interesting to note, since Husserl's philosophy was itself developed largely as an answer to positivism.
42. This was, of course, the situation of Sartre and, among others, of one of his closest friends, P. Nizan. The latter's *The Watchdogs* (New York: Monthly Review Press, 1972) gives a passionate account of the philosophical crisis in France between the world wars.

cally and politically, far too conservative to provide a viable answer to the intellectual and social crisis of the time. Although more philosophically revolutionary, Bergson's philosophy, with its antiintellectualism verging on mysticism, not only shared the socially conservative aspect of Brunschvicg's but appeared unable to provide a realistic philosophical alternative at a time when major scientific and technological changes were seen to form an essential part of the contemporary crisis.

Another important aspect of the situation is that Husserl's philosophy was virtually unknown in France up to the time this book was written. Except for the theologically oriented work of J. Hering,[43] no publication was available in France which presented Husserl's thought "from the inside." Moreover, no more than a handful of publications had even mentioned Husserl's philosophy at all. Those mentions were often made from a biased viewpoint and were based on a very inadequate knowledge of his work. Needless to say, none of Husserl's work was available in translation. The closest approximation to an objective presentation of Husserl's thought was V. Delbos's account of the Prolegomena to the *Logical Investigations*.[44]

In this context, the publication of *Theory of Intuition* (just following Husserl's Paris lectures) had the potential to bring about a major revolution on the French philosophical scene.[45]

As for Levinas, we should note that he himself was limited by the small number of writings that Husserl had allowed for publication (*LU, Ideen I, Phil. als str. Wiss.,* and *Zeitbewusstsein,* which had just been edited by Heidegger).[46] However, Levinas had been a student of Husserl and Heidegger in Freiburg, which allowed him to overcome to some extent such limitations. Yet, in this connection, it is important to remember that, at that time, the philosophical differences between Husserl and Heidegger had not yet become fully apparent. It was difficult (if

43. *Phénoménologie et philosophie religieuse* (Paris: Alcan, 1925).

44. "Husserl: Sa critique du psychologisme et sa conception d'une logique pure," *Revue de métaphysique et de morale,* Vol. XIX (1911).

45. One can obtain a feeling of the revolutionary impact Husserl's philosophy had in France from Jean-Paul Sartre, "Une Idée fondamentale de la phénoménologie de Husserl: L'Intentionalité," *Situations I* (Paris: Gallimard, 1947).

46. I purposely omit from this list *Philosophie der Arithmetik* (Halle: Pfeffer, 1891), which at that time was hardly considered part of the Husserlian "corpus."

not at times impossible) to separate, in what Levinas had learned in Freiburg, Husserl's own teachings from Heidegger's interpretation of them.

These brief historical remarks should help clarify many of the characteristic features of this book. For one thing, it cannot claim to constitute an introduction to Husserl's philosophy as a whole. For another, even though Levinas' intention was clearly to give an "objective" [47] account of Husserl's thought as it was known to him, this book cannot but exhibit a certain Heideggerian bias [48] or escape being in many ways polemical.

This polemic is aimed in three directions. First, it was important to contrast (despite many apparent similarities) Husserl's intuitionism from that of Bergson;[49] at the same time, Husserl's idealism had to be clearly distinguished from that of the contemporary French idealists. Hence, in the first case, Levinas had to emphasize the idealism and intellectualism of Husserl; in the second, he had to emphasize the intuitionistic nature of Husserl's philosophy.[50]

Finally, if Husserl was little known in France at the time he was even less understood. Many misinterpretations of his thought had to be corrected. V. Delbos's article on the Prolegomena had made Husserl appear to many as a logicist, that is, as belonging to the same school of thought as Russell, Frege, and Couturat. Furthermore, this was a line of thought which had apparently been refuted forever by Poincaré. Moreover, what little had transpired from *Ideen* (and from the second volume of *LU*) had been equally misunderstood. For some it represented a return to crude Platonism, while for others it was but a disguised return to psychologism, sensualism, and empiricism.

On all counts, we can see that Levinas' task of presenting Husserl's thought in all its originality was not an easy one.

47. The word "objective" must be understood here in the light of what Levinas himself says (p. xxxiii).

48. I must nevertheless disagree with H. Spiegelberg's assertion that "of the first three book size introductions to the Phenomenological Movement which appeared between 1926 and 1930 [one of which is *Theory of Intuition*] only the lucid account by Jean Hering . . . had phenomenology represented by Husserl" (*The Phenomenological Movement*, 2d ed. [The Hague: Nijhoff, 1965], p. 402).

49. *Ibid.*, p. 399.

50. It is, therefore, obviously not accidental that Levinas chose to center his presentation of Husserl's philosophy around the problem of intuition.

Levinas had to face an audience which was used to thinking in terms of two conflicting philosophies, both of which bore a false resemblance to Husserl's—an audience, moreover, which suffered from something worse than complete lack of knowledge, the greatest ignorance of all: "To think that you know that which you do not."

NOTES ON THE TRANSLATION [51]

AS WE HAVE NOTED, no translation of Husserl's works was available at the time *Theory of Intuition* was written. As a consequence, Levinas had to assemble his own set of terms, which he uses both in his commentary and in his translation of the Husserlian texts he quotes. As we know, assembling such a vocabulary is more than a "mere" matter of translation. The spirit of an interpretation necessarily creeps into one's choice of words.

Today we face a different situation. In English as well as in French, a moderately stable set of phenomenological terms is becoming available. This terminology, however, did not always seem to me congruent with Levinas' own. This created a problem, that of respecting the spirit of Levinas' commentary without unnecessarily confusing the reader familiar with the English phenomenological vocabulary. Some amount of compromise was necessary. Whenever possible, I tried to use familiar expressions. Yet I have, in general, paid more attention to recapturing the flavor of Levinas' own text than to conforming to preexistent terminology.

As to the translation of Husserl's texts, I have, except in the case of *Ideen,* used the existing English translations. All translations from *Ideen* are my own. There were two reasons why I chose not to use the published translation of *Ideen.* First, it is generally recognized as being largely inadequate. Second, I could not use it and still preserve the unity of style and vocabulary between the text and the quotations which characterizes Levinas.

In conclusion, I want to thank all those whose generous help

---

51. A short *Avant-Propos* by Levinas was omitted from this translation and replaced by the above historical remarks more specifically directed to today's English reader.

and support have made this translation possible: H. Dreyfus, who first helped and encouraged me in starting this project; T. Kyle, who carefully and patiently helped me revise my original translation, straightening out numerous awkward or unidiomatic expressions; T. Crikelair for his work in compiling the index; and many others who at one time or other helped in surmounting one or another difficulty. I also want to thank the College of Liberal Arts of the Pennsylvania State University, which provided me with a grant for secretarial help.

ANDRÉ ORIANNE

Bibliographical Note

FOLLOWING ARE THE WORKS of Edmund Husserl which are frequently cited in this book, along with the abbreviations used.

Logische Untersuchungen, 2d ed., Vols. I and II. Halle: Niemeyer, 1913, 1921. [The second part of Vol. II, published in 1921, is referred to by Levinas as Vol. III; thus references to various parts of the work are abbreviated *LU*, I, II, and III, respectively.] Translated by J. N. Findlay. *Logical Investigations*. 2 vols. New York: Humanities Press, 1970.

"Philosophie als strenge Wissenschaft," in *Logos*, I (1910) (abbreviated *Phil. als str. Wiss.*). Translated by Quentin Lauer, in *Edmund Husserl: Phenomenology and the Crisis of Philosophy*. New York: Harper & Row, Harper Torchbook, 1965. Pp. 71–147.

"Ideen zu einer reinen Phänomenologie und phänomenologischen Philosophie," in *Jahrbuch für Philosophie und phänomenologische Forschung*, I (Halle, 1913) (abbreviated as *Ideen*). Translated by W. R. Boyce Gibson. *Ideas*. New York: Macmillan, 1931.

"Husserl's Vorlesungen zur Phänomenologie des inneren Zeitbewusstsein." Edited by M. Heidegger, in *Jahrbuch für Philosophie und phänomenologische Forschung*, X (Halle, 1928) (abbreviated as *Zeitbewusstsein*). Translated by James S. Churchill. *The Phenomenology of Internal Time-Consciousness*. Bloomington: Indiana University Press, 1964.

All quotations from Husserl's works are taken from the English translations except those from *Ideen*, which have been especially translated for this edition. Page references in brackets in the notes are to the English translation of the cited work.

Introduction

THE PHENOMENOLOGICAL MOVEMENT, which dominates German philosophical life now more than ever, was started at the beginning of this century by the work of Edmund Husserl. In 1900–1901 he published the *Logische Untersuchungen* (*Logical Investigations*). The apparent concern of these investigations was limited to the particular problem of the foundation of logic. In raising and solving this problem, however, the investigations introduced a method whose interest and value for philosophy in general did not escape the small but enthusiastic group that immediately formed around the master.

This method, or rather this manner, of philosophizing is the soul of the phenomenological movement.[1] It is practiced by the founder of phenomenology in his books and courses, and it unites such different minds as Husserl, Scheler, and Heidegger.

A method is never merely an instrument made to explore any part of reality. It is not enough to have a purely formal [2] and universally valid idea of the essence of truth in order to determine the means that make us capable of discovering it in the various spheres of being.[3] In order to have access to some domain of being we must, at least according to Husserl, anticipate the

---

1. See Jean Hering, *Phénoménologie et philosophie religieuse* (Paris: Alcan, 1925), pp. 32 ff. It is the first work dealing with phenomenology published in France. See also the "manifesto" of phenomenology at the beginning of the *Jahrbuch für Philosophie und phänomenologische Forschung*, I (1913).
2. *Ideen*, § 153, p. 322, and chap. 6 below.
3. *Ideen*, § 76, p. 144; § 96, p. 200.

"meaning" of the being which is approached.[4] The method of natural sciences may be inefficient in psychology. The *sui generis* character of psychic being may require a method of investigation that conforms to its "meaning." It is probably because of similar preoccupations that Bergson, in his letter to Harald Höffding, insists that it is duration and not intuition which is the starting point of his philosophy.[5] Like Bergson, Husserl had an intuition of his philosophy before he made it a philosophy of intuition.

This does not mean, of course, that, to find a method for a science, one must already possess that science. It follows only that the science of the "meaning" of being is not identical to the knowledge of the properties of being, that the science of the "meaning" of being has a special status, and that it is in some way a priori inasmuch as it is presupposed by the knowledge of the properties of being.[6] Under *ontology* we shall see later a number of a priori sciences coming to the fore,[7] and we shall have occasion more than once to go over the distinction between the study of being and the study of the meaning of being, or ontology.[8] What we must remember at the outset is that any consideration of method goes beyond the framework of a purely formal logic and deep into an ontology.

Our project here is to study intuitionism in Husserl's phenomenology, so we cannot separate in our presentation the theory of intuition as a philosophical method from what may be called Husserl's ontology. We want to show, on the contrary, how the intuition which he proposes as a mode of philosophizing follows from his very conception of being.

Neither our goal nor our method is historical. We do not intend to look for the origin of Husserl's concepts in the history of philosophy. In fact, this would not be easy or even possible. It is not easy to study the history of a doctrine which is too recent for one to have an adequate historical perspective. The other difficulty of making a study which would be historical in its method and aspiration stems from the particular development of Husserl's thought. He came to philosophy through mathe-

---

4. *Phil. als str. Wiss.*, pp. 308–9 [p. 101].
5. See Harald Höffding, *La Philosophie de Bergson*, trans. Jacques de Coussange (Paris: Alcan, 1916), which includes a letter from Bergson to Höffding (p. 160).
6. See below, p. 4.
7. See below, p. 113.
8. See below, pp. 130 ff.

matics,[9] and his thought has evolved in a manner rather independent of historical influences. What appear to be historical influences are often only the result of a congruence with the great classical philosophers. Explicit historical references to philosophers are rare in his works. Husserl's doctrine has constantly evolved, and the numerous unpublished works which are the result of fifteen years of meditation [10] would probably present many surprises to anyone wanting to study phenomenology by the historical method applied to Descartes or Thomas Aquinas. Moreover, such an attempt would be premature, since the last word of Husserl's philosophy may not yet have been spoken— and is certainly not published.

Taking all these circumstances into consideration, we decided on another goal. *We would like to study and present Husserl's philosophy as one studies and presents a living philosophy.* We are not facing a corpus of set propositions from which one can adopt only its rigid forms; we are confronting a living and changing thought in which we must immerse ourselves and philosophize. It is not enough for us to reconstruct Husserl's arguments and follow their skillful web; to put it in a more phenomenological language, we must come face to face with the same "things." We must understand the arguments on the basis of these things rather than try to make them intelligible by means of a text or a premise which may not have been written or formulated.

Under these conditions, the obstacles to a rigorously historical study disappear. The constant evolution of Husserl's philosophy cannot keep us from grasping its simple, main inspiration, which alone makes possible this evolution.

In conformity with our goal, we shall not fear to take into account problems raised by other philosophers, by students of Husserl, and, in particular, by Martin Heidegger,[11] whose influence on this book will often be felt. The intense philosophical life which runs through Heidegger's philosophy sometimes permits us to sharpen the outline of Husserl's philosophy by accentuating some aporias, raising some problems, making certain views more precise, or opposing others. The influence of a

9. See *Philosophie der Arithmetik* (Halle: Pfeffer, 1891). See also the preface to *LU*, I, v [p. 41].

10. See Hering, *Phénoménologie et philosophie religieuse*, p. 35.

11. See Heidegger, "Sein und Zeit," in *Jahrbuch für Philosophie und phänomenologische Forschung*, VIII (1927).

thought on distinguished students seems to allow a more exact grasping of it than would be provided by the laborious studies of a conscientious commentator.

We do not intend to abuse this method. Such a powerful and original philosophy as Heidegger's, even though it is in many respects different from Husserlian phenomenology, is to some extent only its continuation. Given the spirit of our book, which consists in taking into account the inspiration of Husserl's system rather than its history, it seems permissible to use the work done by Husserlian philosophers. Let us give a precise example. Husserl claims that the central problem of transcendental phenomenology, that of the constitution of the world with respect to pure consciousness, introduces a properly philosophical "dimension" into the study of being; [12] this is where the ultimate meaning of reality is revealed to us. What is this ultimate meaning? Why is this a philosophical problem *par excellence*? It seems to us that the problem raised here by transcendental phenomenology is an ontological problem in the very precise sense that Heidegger gives to this term.[13] Knowledge of Heidegger's starting point may allow us to understand better Husserl's end point.[14]

However, the goal of this book prevents us from making a thorough criticism of the philosophy which we shall present. The time has not yet come for that. We prefer to proceed in another way, one which better expresses our attitude toward phenomenology. By simply stating in the course of our presentation the reservations which we have on different points, we shall best express our respect for Husserl's general intentions.

Although we do not concentrate here on the origins of Husserl's doctrine, we must, at least in this Introduction, say something about the philosophical situation in Germany at the moment of the elaboration of the *Logische Untersuchungen*.

In the second half of the nineteenth century, the influence of Hegel's system became neutralized, largely because of the prog-

---

12. *Ideen*, § 62, p. 118; § 63, p. 121. Concerning the search for a "philosophical dimension," see *Phil. als str. Wiss.*, pp. 289–90 [p. 71], and *passim*.

13. Heidegger, "Sein und Zeit."

14. See below, pp. 130, 154–55.

ress of the natural sciences and history.[15] It is generally believed that the sciences exhaust the totality of what can be known of being, so that, at first, philosophy seems to be without an object. But if science knows all that is to be known about being, the sciences themselves may become an object of study. In addition to the knowledge of being, there is room for the knowledge of knowledge—for the theory of knowledge, as it is usually called. This is the place of philosophy, and such a conception of its role and object permits us to understand the fundamental unity of the opposite camps in German philosophy during the second half of the nineteenth century.[16] The naturalist and psychologistic philosophers were identifying philosophy and experimental psychology (Wundt, Erdmann, Sigwart), while the Marburg school (Hermann Cohen, Natorp), Alois Riehl, the school of Windelband, etc., were trying to renew the Kantian critique by interpreting it as a theory of knowledge. Common to all these philosophers is the identification of philosophy and theory of knowledge, the latter being understood as a reflection on the sciences. While the antipsychologists were giving a special dignity to the theory of knowledge, to "transcendental philosophy," above that of the natural sciences, the psychologists were claiming that this reflection on the sciences had to be itself a science of nature and had to use the same methods as physics or chemistry; in short, that empirical psychology had to be the foundation of a theory of knowledge and logic, the only two philosophical disciplines. This same general tendency of the times helps us understand why Dilthey and Windelband were questioning the method of the *Geisteswissenschaften.* To them, it was merely a question of completing Kant's theory of knowledge, which was only a theory of the knowledge of nature, with a similar theory for the sciences of the mind. Here, also, the only remaining problem of philosophy is that of the theory of knowledge. Even Husserl, at least from time to time, does not escape this conception of philosophy.

15. Husserl is probably thinking of the Hegelian system when he speaks of these "spekulativen Konstruktionen, durch welche der naturwissenschaftsfremde Idealismus in der ersten Hälfte des 19. Jahrhunderts die echte Wissenschaft so sehr gehemmt habe" (*Ideen*, § 19, p. 35).

16. We owe this connection to a course given by Heidegger in the winter term, 1928–29.

However, as we shall try to show, his philosophy goes beyond an epistemological viewpoint.[17]

We shall show here that, as early as the first volume [18] of the *Logische Untersuchungen*, in which Husserl is mainly concerned with fighting psychologism, he has deeper intentions. The real reason that Husserl attacks psychologism, a reason which explains all the others, is that psychologism presupposes a theory of being. At least implicitly, psychologism is itself founded on a more general philosophy which has a definite way of interpreting the structure of being. It is founded on an ontology, and this ontology is naturalism. Hence, after going beyond psychologism in logic, Husserl went even further. He extended his critique to the whole of psychologistic ontology and looked not only for a new logic but for a new philosophy.[19]

Since we want to know how intuition follows from Husserl's theory of being, and the role intuition plays there, it will be easy for us to throw light on this theory by opposing it to psychologism.

Therefore we shall begin by presenting psychologism and naturalism as conceived by Husserl (chapter 1). We are not especially concerned with Husserl's logic. His critique of psychologism in Volume I of the *Logische Untersuchungen* matters to us, not *qua* contribution to the discussion between logicism and psychologism, but because his presentation of psychologism illustrates the philosophy on which it is based.

We shall next see how naturalistic philosophy is overcome by Husserl and how he reaches a new conception of being (chapters 2 and 3). The latter will make it intelligible that intuition, understood as the theoretical act (chapter 4) of consciousness that makes objects present to us, is not only a mode of knowledge among others but is the original phenomenon which makes truth itself possible (chapters 5 and 6). Finally, we shall see the philosophical dimension which is opened by this new theory of being, and thereby the value and sense of this privileged type of intuition: immanent intuition, philosophical intuition (chapter 7).

17. See below, p. 130.
18. French readers may know its content through a summary by Victor Delbos, "Husserl: Sa Critique du psychologisme et sa conception d'une logique pure," in *Revue de métaphysique et de morale*, Vol. XIX (1911).
19. See the foreword to the 2d ed., *LU*, I, viii ff. [pp. 43 ff.].

The Theory of Intuition
in Husserl's Phenomenology

1 / The Naturalistic Theory
of Being and the
Method of Philosophy

BEFORE PRESENTING NATURALISM as it is conceived, criticized, and superseded by Husserl, we must make a few remarks (which will be clarified later). They will show on what grounds Husserl comes to grips with and fights the profound principle of naturalism. Naturalism, as we have said, is a general philosophy, a theory of being. Hence, in anticipation of our conclusions, we must now explain in what respects being can be the object of a theory.

First, being is the object of such sciences as physics, biology, psychology, etc. These sciences, however, make use of a certain number of fundamental notions whose meaning the sciences themselves do not clarify—for example, memory, perception, space, time, etc. These notions determine the necessary structure of different domains of being and constitute their essence.[1] Hence a theory of being could adopt a viewpoint from which, in some way, it would study *being qua being* by considering the categories which are the conditions of the very existence of being. A theory of being would then become an ontology.

However, the Husserlian conception of ontology has the particular feature that the structure of being which is the object of ontology is not everywhere the same: diverse *regions* of being (*Seinsregionen*) have a different constitution and cannot be thought of by means of the same categories.[2] Some notions, such as those of *object, relation, property*, etc., have, of course, a uni-

1. See below, pp. 113 ff.
2. See below, p. 115.

versal applicability. But the structure expressed by those concepts which are common to all regions of being is purely formal. According to Husserl, formal concepts, such as that of *object in general,* do not form a superior genus of which all the others would be but species. One must distinguish between genus and form,[3] because the universality of a form transcends all generality. The categories which express the material (*sachhaltige*) structure of being, which define nature as nature and consciousness as consciousness, are not simply specifications of formal categories (the results of adding the *differentia specifica* to the *genus proximum*).[4] The ontology which describes the essence of space, causality, materiality, and, in the domain of consciousness, the essence of will, sensibility, etc., is not a particular instance of the science of forms which Husserl calls *formal ontology.* These material—ontological, in the proper sense of the term—categories are different in each domain of being. They divide, as Husserl expresses it, existence into *regions.* Each region is the object of a *regional ontology.*

But for Husserl, the study of being is not exhausted by the natural sciences and the regional ontologies.

As one of our conclusions we will establish the following: the regions of being differ from each other not only in their essences and in the categories which delimit their essences but also in their existence. The very fact of being, of being there, is not an empty and uniform characteristic, superimposed on essences which alone would have the privilege of being able to differ from one another. *To exist does not mean the same thing in every region.*

This thesis, in our opinion one of the most interesting in phenomenology, seems to come out of all of Husserl's philosophy. We shall try to show this in detail later. We can only mention here the new ontological problem [5] which arises when we study not only the essence of being but also its existence, and *what it means that an object be.*[6]

Let us take advantage of this brief presentation of the con-

3. See *Ideen,* § 13, pp. 26–27.
4. *Ibid.,* p. 27.
5. It is clear that the term *ontology* must not be understood here—or in the rest of our work—in the sense which it had in the eighteenth century. It should not be identified with the term *metaphysics.*
6. See *Phil. als str. Wiss.,* p. 301 [p. 90].

cept and problems of ontology to speak, in the light of the distinctions that we have just established, of naturalistic philosophy. We must ask what type of existence naturalism attributes to being, and by means of what categories naturalism conceives of being.

We will show later how *existence* may become the object of phenomenological investigation; let us remark, for the time being, that if the existence of an object may become accessible to us it can only be through the knowledge of what this existence means for us. "The true concept of the *transcendence of a thing,*[7] which is the measure of any reasonable assertion about transcendence, can only be found in the essential content of perception or of those determinate structures which we call evidential experiences [*ausweisende Erfahrung*]."[8] We shall see later[9] that these propositions follow from the whole of Husserl's philosophy. We must conclude that, in order to grasp the specific mode of existence of physical nature, we will have to analyze the intrinsic and irreducible meaning of the experience of the physical world. What is its mode of appearing, of presenting itself to consciousness, and of asserting itself as existing?

Nature reveals itself in successive apparitions, in multiple, changing, subjective phenomena (*subjektive Erscheinungen*). A material thing is given to us through many aspects and perspectives, under many different lights, etc. "A thing is . . . an object which is given to consciousness as one and identical in the continuous and regular flux of the multiple perceptions which flow into each other."[10] "It can only appear from a certain angle, in which are already inscribed systematic possibilities of ever new perspectives."[11]

When we call the aspects and perspectives, the light, etc., under which an object appears "subjective," it does not mean that these are subjective *contents* of consciousness or that they are in some way the components of consciousness.[12] We call them "subjective" to oppose them to a stable and immutable ideal of objectivity, an objectivity that would be indifferent to

---

7. My italics.
8. *Ideen,* § 47, p. 89; see also § 44, p. 80.
9. See below, chap. 2.
10. *Ideen,* § 41, p. 75.
11. *Ibid.,* § 42, p. 78; see also p. 77: "Das Ding nehmen wir dadurch wahr, dass es sich abschattet."
12. *Ibid.,* § 41, p. 73.

the very existence of a subjectivity. But it also means connecting them with subjectivity, a connection to which we will have to return later. This connection is certainly not a relation between container and contained. Within each of these subjective phenomena we distinguish a subjective act, an immanent psychological content, and an objective sphere of which this act of consciousness is conscious.[13] Even though this side of the table which is offered to sight is only a subjective view of an objective table, immutable in space and time, it is in no way a content of consciousness but rather its object.

No matter how fluid a series of subjective phenomena, it gives the intimation of a stable and objective *thing* which claims to have an independent existence transcending the flux of perception. This is the second characteristic of the experience of material objects. When we see one side of an object, the whole object is intimated as something which, through the relativity, multiplicity, and constant changing of its subjective appearances, presents itself as "the temporal unity of enduring or changing properties." [14]

The duality in the experience of a material thing that we have just observed has a *sui generis* structure. The subjective phenomena are not given as distinct from the object they intimate. Their relation is not comparable to that of a sign or an image to the thing they signify or represent. The subjective phenomena of a thing are not its images or its signs, which an intelligence more powerful than ours might have bypassed in order to reach directly a *thing in itself*.[15] If we follow step by step the internal meaning of the experience of a material thing, we must recognize that the thing intimated in perception is everything it is solely by virtue of being intimated in perception. Things are given as an ideal that the rest of the experience tends to realize but whose existence consists precisely in being the ideal of these changing perceptions.[16] "Spatial things are nothing but an intentional unity which, in principle, cannot be given otherwise than as the unity of such phenomena." [17] Besides, it is not enough to admit that the things which appear are not independent of their appearance; we must also admit a certain iden-

13. *Ibid.*, § 41, pp. 73–74; § 42, p. 76; § 52, p. 97.
14. See *Phil. als str. Wiss.*, p. 310 [p. 104].
15. See *Ideen*, § 43, pp. 78–79; § 52, pp. 97, 102.
16. *Ibid.*, § 143, p. 297; *Phil. als str. Wiss.*, p. 311 [p. 105].
17. *Ideen*, § 42, p. 78; see also *Phil. als str. Wiss.*, p. 311 [p. 105].

tity between the two. In some sense each appearance contains the *whole* thing. We perceive a thing "in a *continuous perceptual series*, feeling it over as it were with our senses. But each single percept in this series is already a percept of the thing." [18]

Let us explicitly state that it is inherent in the very essence of material things that they should appear through a multiplicity of *Abschattungen* (perspectives, one-sided views).

> If *our* perception can reach things themselves only by means of mere *Abschattungen*, it is neither because of a contingent whim of things nor because of an accident of *our human constitution*. It is . . . evident, and it follows from the essence of spatial things . . . that a being so structured can, in principle, only be given through *Abschattungen*.[19]

But the meaning of the experience of the material world is not exhausted by this relation between the subjective phenomena and the unity they constitute. The thing, as the ideal which is intimated by the unilateral perspectives of perception, bears in turn the marks of relativity and simultaneously refers back to the superior ideal of absolute being. The unities of which the subjective phenomena are only unilateral perspectives, the objective things that are intimated, present themselves as "incorporated in the totality of one corporeal world, that binds them all together with its one space and its one time." [20] It is the physicist who, driven by the inherent relativity of immediate experience, tries to overcome it by constructing, on the basis of these *pure appearances* of our concrete life, the transcendent world of physical science.

The manner in which this world is built by scientific thought is guided by the actual content of the concrete world. "Realities," says Husserl,

> are given as unities of immediate experience, as unities of diverse sensible appearances [*Erscheinungen*]. Stabilities, changes and relationships of change (all of which can be grasped sensibly) direct cognition everywhere, and function for it like a "vague" medium in which the true, objective, physically exact nature presents itself, a medium through which thought (as empirically scientific thought) determines and constructs [*herausbestimmt, herauskonstituiert*] what is true.[21]

18. *LU*, III, 148–49 [p. 789].
19. *Ideen*, § 42, p. 77.
20. *Phil. als str. Wiss.*, p. 311 [p. 104].
21. *Ibid.* [pp. 104–5].

Elsewhere he writes: "What is given in perception is used in the rigorous method of the sciences, to determine . . . this transcendent being." [22]

The physical world "is a unity of spatiotemporal being subject to exact laws of nature." [23] Notions such as that of atom, ion, etc., take the place of sensible and concrete qualities.[24] The whole of reality so constituted is governed by the law of causality. In the concrete but *subjective* world of experience we are dealing with things. In the ideal but *objective* world of science it is the convergence of causal chains which constitute things, the substances underlying properties. The properties of things, far from being the nature or essence of things, are nothing but possible lines of causality. Things

> are what they are only in this unity [of nature]; only in the causal relation to or connection with each other do they retain their individual identity (substance), ... Every corporeal being is subject to laws of possible changes, and these laws concern the identical, the thing, not by itself but in the unified, actual and possible totality of the one nature. Each physical thing has its nature . . . by virtue of being the union point of causalities within the one all-nature. Real properties (real after the manner of things, corporeal) are a title for the possibilities of transformation of something identical, possibilities preindicated according to the laws of causality. And thus this identical [thing], with regard to what it is, is determinable only by recourse to these laws.[25]

Natural sciences do nothing but try to reach this ideal of objectivity that is already intimated in concrete perception. They

22. *Ideen,* § 40, p. 73; see also § 52, pp. 100–101. This interpretation of the method of science, which amounts to the construction of a physical reality from subjective appearances, reminds one to some extent of the ideas of E. Goblot (see his article, "Qu'est-ce que le réel?" in *Revue de l'université de Bruxelles,* Vol. XXXII [October–November, 1927]).

However, let us say explicitly that the resemblance is limited to this construction in science. The problems of phenomenological constitution that we shall discuss later are quite different and reflect a different philosophical interest. Even if Husserl agrees with Goblot on the description of the method of science, he interprets it differently. For Husserl, it is the subjective world which is real; the physical world has reality of another degree. The idea of intentionality allows Husserl to attribute "objectivity" to the "subjective" world.

23. *Phil. als str. Wiss.,* p. 294 [p. 79].
24. *Ideen,* § 40, p. 72.
25. *Phil. als str. Wiss.,* p. 311 [p. 104].

try to overcome the vagueness and approximation of the naïve
experience of perception, to reach the world which is intimated
by that of our concrete life and which allows us to orient ourselves in it.[26] Husserl explicitly admits that

> Natural science, then, simply follows consistently the sense of
> what the thing pretends to be as experienced and calls this—
> vaguely enough—"elimination of secondary qualities," "elimina-
> tion of the merely subjective in the appearance," while retaining
> what is left, the primary qualities.[27]

There is already in this last quotation the beginning of a
criticism, or at least the indication of a certain lack of clarity.
The scientist is mistaken as soon as he tries, in his own way, to
interpret what he is doing.[28] Naturalism seems to be only a bad
interpretation of the meaning of natural science.

Indeed, we have seen that, in the world constructed by science, the substance of things is reduced to a convergence of
causal chains. It is thus asserted that, within this constructed
world, *to exist* means to belong to nature and to be subsumed
under its categories, such as time, space, and causality; and, of
course, time, space, and causality are here meant as they are
understood in the formulae of the physicist, that is, in a way
which transcends concrete time, space, and causality, this *vague
medium* in which our life takes place.[29]

By asserting the objectivity of the physical world, naturalism
identifies the existence and the conditions of existence of the
physical world with existence and the conditions of existence in
general. It forgets that the world of the physicist necessarily refers back, through its intrinsic meaning,[30] to the "subjective"
world which one tries to exclude from reality as being pure appearance, conditioned by the empirical nature of man—which is
incapable of reaching directly to a world of *things in themselves*.[31] *But while the world of the physicist claims to go beyond
naïve experience, his world really exists only in relation to naïve
experience*. This would be true even of a divine physics.[32]

26. *Ideen*, § 40, p. 73.
27. *Phil. als str. Wiss.*, p. 311 [p. 105]; *Ideen*, § 47, pp. 87–88.
28. *Ideen*, § 25, p. 44; § 52, p. 97; and *passim*.
29. *Ibid.*, § 49, p. 92; § 40, pp. 71–72.
30. *Ibid.*, § 52, pp. 98, 101.
31. *Ibid.*, pp. 97–98.
32. *Ibid.*, p. 102.

This was suggested above when we discussed a certain identity between appearances and things. What physics studies is already aimed at in a certain way, in perception.

> Physical objects are not something foreign to the objects which appear *in person* in sensible experience, but are intimated by them and, a priori, solely by them for essential and immutable reasons. We must add that the sensible determining content of this X which functions as support of the determinations of physicists is not a disguise foreign to these determinations, nor does it hide them; rather, it is only in as much as this X is the subject of sensible determinations that it can also be subject of the determinations of physicists which, for their part, *are intimated* by the sensible determinations. In principle, a thing, and in particular the things about which the physicists talk, can only be given in a sensible manner, in sensible modes of appearing . . . ; and the identical object which appears in the changing continuity of these modes is this object itself which the physicist . . . submits to a causal analysis, to a search for real necessary connexions.[33]

Consequently, where natural science is still right, naturalism is already wrong. By interpreting the ideal world which is discovered by science on the basis of the changing and elusive world of perception as absolute being, of which the perceptible world would be only a subjective appearance,[34] naturalism betrays the internal meaning of perceptual experience. Physical nature has meaning only with respect to an existence which is revealed through the relativity of *Abschattungen*—and this is the *sui generis* mode of existing of material reality.

But naturalism, which misinterprets the meaning of the existence of nature itself, believes that in the nature revealed by physical science it reaches absolute being,[35] and it consistently reduces the totality of being to nature.[36] "The natural scientist has the tendency to look upon everything as nature and . . . so to falsify the sense of what cannot be seen . . . [his] way."[37]

A spiritual or ideal existence must be part of nature in order really to be.

33. *Ibid.*, pp. 99–100; see also the entire § 52, beginning on p. 97.
34. *Ibid.*, pp. 97–98.
35. *Ibid.*, p. 101.
36. *Ibid.*, § 19, p. 35.
37. *Phil. als str. Wiss.*, p. 294 [p. 79].

Every psychological determination is by that very fact psychophysical, . . . *it has a never-failing physical connotation.*[38] Even where psychology—the empirical science—concerns itself with determinations of bare events of consciousness and not with dependences that are psychophysical in the usual and narrower sense, those events are thought of, nevertheless, as belonging to nature, that is, as belonging to human or brute consciousness that for their part have an unquestioned and coapprehended connection with human and brute organisms. To eliminate the relation to nature would deprive the psychical of its character as an objectively and temporally determinable fact of nature.[39]

The naturalist . . . sees only nature, and primarily physical nature. Whatever is, is either itself physical, belonging to the unified totality of physical nature, or it is in fact psychical, but then merely as a variable dependent on the physical, at best a secondary "parallel accompaniment." [40]

The deeper sense of these passages does more than attribute to naturalism the theses of materialism. The fault Husserl finds in naturalism is not purely metaphysical: naturalism is not a metaphysical theory which would take matter and mind as two existing beings and, without inquiring into the mode of existence of each of these beings, would wonder only about their mutual dependence or independence. True, naturalism asks these metaphysical questions, and it is only too often materialistic. But the manner in which we have set the problem has shown that we mean to attack the very type of existence which, for naturalism —at least implicitly—is the very meaning of *being*. From this point of view, the passages we have cited are interesting in a different way. They demonstrate that, according to Husserl, the very objectivity of a psychic phenomenon implies, for naturalism, the existence of the physical world. Being, for naturalism, may not mean having a material existence, but it at least means *being there* in the same way that the material world is, being on the same level as it. To think of something as existing is to think of something in physical nature and, consequently, having the same mode of existence as physical nature does. Objectivity, reality, existence would vanish if one were to take away from a psychic phenomenon the fact of its belonging to nature.

38. My italics.
39. *Phil. als str. Wiss.*, pp. 298–99 [p. 86].
40. *Ibid.*, p. 294 [p. 79].

This is the true origin of naturalism: naturalism conceives the existence of the whole of being on the model of material things. It understands the manner of appearing and of being revealed of the whole of being in the same way as it understands that of a material thing. A material thing is intimated through experienced subjective phenomena [41] in which it offers itself as an absolute reality. We can now understand Husserl's assertion that naturalism remains what it is in an idealistic philosophy as well as in a realistic philosophy:

> Whatever is belongs to psychophysical nature. . . . From our point of view, there is no essential alteration in this interpretation, when . . . physical nature is sensualistically broken up into complementary complexes of sensations, into colors, sounds, pressures, etc., and in the same way the so-called "psychical" is broken up into complementary complexes of the same or still other "sensations." [42]

In both philosophies, to be is to be like inert matter.

It is in this *ontological* identification of consciousness and matter—to use a term which we have already explained—that the deeper and truer root of the materialization, of the *naturalization*, of the *reification* of consciousness, lies. And this reification will be unavoidable, despite any attempt to conceive the essence of consciousness as different from the essence of material things, as long as the concept of *existence* is not extended. Whether one puts consciousness beside the physical world or resolves the physical world into contents of consciousness, in either case consciousness and the physical world coexist in nature and have an identical way of revealing themselves and of existing.

It is also this concept of existence that forces us to naturalize the subjective phenomena and the essences of the physical world —a naturalization which has been made possible through the naturalization of consciousness. As long as the existence of consciousness cannot be conceived differently, psychologism, the naturalization of concepts, will be unavoidable. This is why the critique of psychologism in Volume I of the *Logische Untersuchungen*, which begins by distinguishing essences from the psychological act which conceives essences, is necessarily led to study the essence of consciousness and, as we shall show, its mode of existing. Whereas some critics have thought they could

41. *Ideen*, § 19, p. 35.
42. *Phil. als str. Wiss.*, p. 294 [pp. 79–80].

accuse Husserl of a relapse into psychologism,[43] quite the contrary is true: Volume II of the *Logische Untersuchungen* builds a new ontology of consciousness to replace naturalistic ontology, and this ontology has been mistaken for psychologism.

Let us now follow the stages of this naturalization of consciousness, starting from the naturalistic idea of existence that is its moving force. If to be is to be in nature, then consciousness, through which nature is known, must also be a part of nature inasmuch as it claims to exist. Otherwise it would be nothing. But then we must apply to consciousness the same categories as are applied to physical nature, namely, time, space (inasmuch as consciousness is always conceived as being bound to bodies and organs), and causality. This psychic world is not isolated in nature; it is connected to the material world through the bodies of men and animals, and there is a causal interaction between the two worlds.

In this manner, consciousness has the same existence as nature. It is a reality in an ideal space and time whose concrete life is but a subjective manifestation, behind which one would have to look for its constituent elements.[44]

We have distinguished the multiplicity of the subjective phenomena, which necessarily belong to the experience of nature, from the multiplicity of the acts of consciousness which are directed toward it. But this distinction, which we have made through a reflection on the internal meaning of the experience of nature, is not consistent with the naturalistic notion of being, since naturalism understands this very experience in the light of the being which it intimates. If the experience of nature is anything at all, it must be a part of nature. Since it is obviously not a part of material nature, it must be a part of psychic nature. The subjective phenomena of objects are the constitutive elements of consciousness—its contents.[45] At the same time, the relation between these subjective phenomena and the reality they intimate is interpreted as a causal relationship—the only relationship admitted by naturalism. Sensations, perceptions, and ideas are the result of a causal action of reality on consciousness.[46] Knowledge can only be a causal process between material beings and psychic beings; both are part of the same nature.

43. *LU*, III, v [p. 662].
44. See *Phil. als str. Wiss.*, p. 310 [p. 103].
45. See *Ideen*, § 52, p. 101.
46. *Ibid.*

Besides consciousness, naturalism is also obliged to naturalize everything which is either ideal or general [47]—numbers, geometrical essences, etc.—if it wants to attribute to them any reality at all. Nature's type of reality is indeed individual. It is individualized in time and made accessible through sensible experience (internal or external). If anything general exists, it must be in some way individual, since it must be part of nature. But nature is the world outside of consciousness and, once consciousness has been naturalized, it too is part of nature. Since ideal objects apparently do not exist in external nature, they must be found in consciousness.[48] Hence general objects can be only contents of conscious life and thus individual objects having individual properties.[49] Their ideality cannot be a mode of existence that belongs to their own nature but can only be a property of the psychological states to which ideal objects are reduced. One can thus understand [50] the existence of those theories of abstraction that are so frequent in naturalism, the theories of Locke, Berkeley, Hume, etc.[51] They are all confronted with what seems to them inconceivable: [52] an ideal existence. Their problem consists in reducing the ideality of an object to a content of psychological life. Let us note again that the naturalization of consciousness is the condition of the naturalization of essences.[53] Indeed, we shall see that, once the former has been overcome, we shall be able to rehabilitate essences.[54]

However, we do not think only of ideal objects but also of the laws founded on those objects, such as mathematical laws. The deduction of Pythagoras' theorem is founded in the essences of a right triangle, square, etc. It is because of the nature of one or another premise that we can, in a syllogism, derive a conclusion. To account for this, naturalism, which denies the existence of essences, need only follow its own line of thought to its ultimate conclusion. Since essences are psychological, natural facts, whatever relation exists between them can only be the relation

47. *Ibid.*, § 18, p. 34.
48. *LU*, II, 123 [p. 351].
49. *Ideen*, § 22, p. 41; § 61, p. 116.
50. *Ibid.*, § 22, p. 41.
51. See Husserl's criticisms of them in *LU*, II, 106–224 [pp. 337–432].
52. *Ibid.*, p. 107 [p. 337].
53. *Ibid.*, pp. 160–62 [pp. 381–83].
54. See below, chap. 6.

common to all natural facts—the relation of causality. Mathematical and logical conclusions are the products of their premises in the same manner as water is produced by the union of hydrogen and oxygen.[55]

We have just presented the psychologistic consequences of naturalism. If philosophy—as the naturalists hold—has the study of knowledge as its sole object, it can be identified with psychology, which in turn is considered one of the natural sciences. Logic can be only an art which is based on that part of psychology which studies the laws of thought.[56] As for the problem of knowledge, psychologism places subject and object in the same world, which it calls nature, and studies their relation as a relation of causality. In order to know how a subject reaches an object which transcends it, one must look for causes which bring about knowledge: excitations of sensory organs by external objects, reflexes, reactions of the organism, etc. When naturalism is idealistic—which does not change its essence—it becomes a question of knowing how the flux of consciousness is produced, those causes inside the flux that must come into play, etc., so that evidence appears at a certain moment in this flux; this evidence, for psychologism, is only a feeling and is void of any objective value.[57] The whole of conscious life is only a flux of inert states, of psychic atoms; evidence is an atom among other atoms. Truth is only this feeling of evidence.

For such a conception of philosophy, the only possible method is that of the natural sciences: "experience," in the precise scientific sense of the term. We have described its essential procedure. It does not consist in simply grasping what is given in perception. We have seen that the specific being of nature imposes the search, in the midst of a multiple and changing reality, for a causality which is *behind* it. One must start from what is immediately given and go back to that reality which accounts for what is given. The movement of science is not so much the passage from the particular to the general as it is the passage from the concrete sensible to the hypothetical superstructure which claims to realize what is intimated in the subjective phenomena. In other words: *the essential movement of a truth-oriented thought consists in the construction of a supremely real world*

55. *LU*, I, 102–9 [pp. 129–34].
56. *Ibid.*, p. 51 [p. 90], and *passim*.
57. *Ibid.*, pp. 180 ff. [pp. 398 ff.]; *Ideen*, § 145, p. 300.

on the basis of the concrete world in which we live. This method is the rejection of everything that is immediate, concrete, and irreducible in direct perception. Because the world of perception is given as relative, because it refers back to a reality which would be behind it, this perception has no scientific value and serves only as a point of departure for a process of reasoning which would have to construct the real world while accounting for appearances, since the latter give themselves as something which must be accounted for.

If, by *intuition*, one roughly understands immediate and direct knowledge, then for naturalism intuition cannot be a scientific method, because what is immediate is only apparent.

We can see now the path that we should follow. We have shown how naturalism has founded a certain conception of scientific and philosophical method—and we have shown that the very heart of naturalism from which everything follows is its conception of existence. We must now ask how Husserl's phenomenology, as it overcomes naturalistic ontology, also leads to another conception of the philosophical method and of truth in general.

2 / The Phenomenological Theory of Being: The Absolute Existence of Consciousness

IF *to be* means to exist the way nature does, then everything which is given as refractory to the categories and to the mode of existence of nature will, as such, have no objectivity and will be, a priori and unavoidably, reduced to something natural. The characteristics of such objects will be reduced to purely subjective phenomena which, with their multifarious structure, are the products of natural causality. Let us illustrate this with an example. The beauty which is manifested in an aesthetic experience presents itself as belonging to the realm of objectivity. The beauty of a work of art is not simply a "subjective feeling" occasioned by such and such properties of the work which, in itself, is beyond beauty or ugliness. *Aesthetic objects themselves are beautiful*—at least this is the intrinsic meaning of an aesthetic experience. But this object, value, or beauty, with its *sui generis* mode of existence, is incompatible with the categories applied to it by naturalism.[1] If it is granted that these categories are the only norms of reality, then naturalism, which attempts to reduce whatever is real in an aesthetic experience to such categories, could possibly preserve the meaning of such an experience, but this experience would still be considered as being intrinsically a psychological phenomenon in nature. As long as the naturalistic ontology is accepted, existence, including the existence of nature, is not determined by the meaning of life. Rather, life itself must, in order to exist, be conceived on the model of nature. That is, life must be integrated in causal chains and

1. *Ideen,* § 152, p. 318.

[17]

granted reality only inasmuch as it belongs to them. The intrinsic meaning of this experience would be only a property, a phenomenon among others. Faithful to its principle, naturalism reduces the meaning of acts of consciousness, no matter how original or irreducible,[2] to nature, which alone really exists. Naturalistic descriptions have a descriptive value, but they cannot be used to derive any assertion concerning the existence of values. Beauty, in our example, is real only *qua* psychological phenomenon within the causal course of nature. A descriptive psychology cannot by itself go beyond naturalism.

Therefore, in order to go conclusively beyond naturalism and all its consequences,[3] it is not enough to appeal to descriptions which emphasize the particular character, irreducible to the naturalistic categories, of certain objects. It is necessary to dig deeper, down to the very meaning of the notion of being, and to show that the origin of all being, including that of nature, is determined by the intrinsic meaning of conscious life and not the other way around. It is only then that the descriptions which deal with the intrinsic meaning of consciousness, descriptions which must be provided by intuition, will have more than a merely psychological value. On this depends the philosophical standing of intuition. It is not without reason that Husserl saw the main failing of the first edition of the *Logische Untersuchungen* in the fact that, in the introduction to Volume II, he had characterized phenomenology as descriptive psychology.[4]

We must therefore determine which theory of being may, negatively, detach itself from the naturalistic ideal of existence and may, positively, rely solely on the internal meaning of life.

The preceding chapter has already carried us some distance in that direction. Indeed, we have tried to show how the world of physical science, whose absolute rights are proclaimed by the physicist, refers essentially to a series of subjective phenomena. We have also emphasized that this relation to subjectivity must not be understood as a relation between container and contained, and that it would be premature to see here a new form of Berkeleian idealism. Nevertheless, some relation to subjectivity is in-

2. *Ibid.*, § 19, p. 36.
3. Concerning the motives which led Husserl to criticize and go beyond naturalism, see *ibid.*, § 18, pp. 33–34.
4. Husserl, "Bericht über deutsche Schriften zur Logik in den Jahren 1895–99," *Archiv für systematische Philosophie*, X (1903), 397–400; *LU*, foreword to the 2d ed., p. xiii [p. 47]; *Ideen*, § 49, p. 92.

herent in the very meaning of these subjective phenomena. The different sides of a table that are successively discovered from different points of view in some way presuppose a consciousness capable of orienting itself. We will postpone the study of this relation,[5] but all our analyses lead us to say, with Husserl, that "the world of transcendent *res* necessarily depends on [*ist ange-wiesen an*] consciousness." [6]

Someone may object that material things extend beyond the realm of our present perception. It belongs to their very essence to be more than what is intimated or revealed in a continuum of subjective aspects at the moment of perception. They are also there when we do not perceive them: they exist in themselves. Is it then possible to find a necessary connection between the mode of existing of material objects and a continuous series of "subjective phenomena"?

Husserl recognizes that the independence from instantaneous perception exhibited by material things is not merely an illusion. But he thinks that he is able to account for this within the framework of a theory which puts external things in a necessary relation to consciousness.

The concept of consciousness includes more than the central sphere of awakened and active consciousness. Husserl is far from ignoring that—as had been perceived by Bergson and James—each moment of consciousness is surrounded by a halo, by fringes, or, in Husserl's terms, by *horizons*, which are, so to speak, in the margin of the central phenomenon: [7] "Each perception is an *ex-ception* [*jedes Erfassen ist ein Herausfassen*]." [8] Cogitation makes the *cogitatum* its own by extracting it from a background which constantly accompanies it and which may become itself the object of an *Herausfassung*.[9] In the latter case, what was originally kept in sight falls into the background without totally disappearing from the field of consciousness. In a new *cogito*, "the preceding *cogito* ceases to shine, falls in the darkness, but is still kept alive, although in a different manner." [10] It

5. See below, chap. 3.

6. *Ideen,* § 49, p. 92.

7. We shall see later how, despite the "continuity" of the various moments of consciousness and despite those fringes which make impossible any exact delimitation of psychic life, Husserl has not condemned the intellect. See chap. 6.

8. *Ideen.,* § 35, p. 62.

9. *Ibid.,* § 113, pp. 230–31.

10. *Ibid.,* § 115, p. 236.

may remain, in certain cases, as the mere possibility of our going back to it, a possibility implicitly contained in each present moment.

The opposition between central and marginal consciousness is not proper to perception alone, and its manifestation in the guise of *Herausfassung* by one's attention is but a particular case of it. It can be found in all the acts of consciousness: acts of memory, imagination, pleasure, will, etc.[11] In the background of conscious life there is a multitude of cogitations. This background is not a vagueness beyond the reaches of analysis, a sort of fog within consciousness; it is a field already differentiated. One can distinguish in it various types of acts: acts of belief (the dawning of a genuine belief, a belief that precedes knowledge etc.),[12] of pleasure or displeasure, of desire, etc. Something like tentative acts are present before the acts themselves: tentative judgments, pleasure, desire, etc.[13] There are even decisions of this type which are present "before our accomplishment of a genuine *cogito,* before our ego becomes active by judging, being pleased, desiring or willing."[14]

Without going into the details of this structure, we can oppose actual consciousness to the sphere of possibilities which are contained implicitly in the actual life of consciousness and form a not-yet-actualized or *potential* consciousness.[15]

With the help of the notion of actual and potential consciousness, we can understand the independence shown by the material world with respect to subjectivity. *It is an independence only with respect to actual consciousness.* The object which we do not have actually in sight does not disappear from consciousness. It is given potentially as the object of a possible actual consciousness. "Horizons," as Husserl calls them, in the form of marginal phenomena or in the more indeterminate form of implicit possibilities of consciousness, accompany that which is given clearly and explicitly. We may let our sight wander around these horizons, illuminating certain aspects of them and letting others fall into darkness. *The property of the world of things of being "in itself" means nothing else than this possibility of going*

11. *Ibid.,* § 35, pp. 62–63.
12. *Ibid.,* § 115, p. 236.
13. *Ibid.,* § 84, p. 169.
14. *Ibid.,* § 115, p. 236.
15. *Ibid.,* § 35, p. 63.

back to the same thing and reidentifying it.[16] This conception is of even greater philosophical interest because the potential sphere does not belong to consciousness contingently but as a necessary part of its structure, and so does the possibility for the various moments of the potential sphere to become actual and to be, in turn, surrounded by potentialities. "The flux of consciousness cannot be made of pure actuality."[17] It is necessary "that a continuous and progressive chain of cogitations be always surrounded by a sphere of inactuality which is always ready to become actual."[18]

In summary, the existence of an unperceived material thing can only be its capability of being perceived. This capability is not an empty possibility in the sense that everything that is not contradictory is possible; rather, it is a possibility[19] which belongs to the very essence of consciousness. The existence of the totality of physical reality which forms the background of what is actually perceived represents the positive possibility of the appearance of subjective phenomena of a certain type, an appearance which can be anticipated to a certain extent through the meaning of that which is actually perceived.

> To say that it [the material object] is there, means that starting from the present perceptions, with their effectively apprehended background, some sequence of possible perceptions . . . lead to those sets of perceptions in which the object could appear and be perceived.[20]

So far we have spoken of the existence of the physical objects relative to consciousness. Now we want to make clearer another character of their existence. Not only is their existence relative to a multiplicity of aspects in which they are intimated but, moreover, these aspects never exhaust things: by right, their number is infinite. The aspects which we see at any given mo-

16. *Ibid.*, § 45, p. 84; § 47, p. 89.
17. *Ibid.*, § 35, p. 63.
18. *Ibid.*, p. 64.
18. *Ibid.*, p. 64.
19. Concerning the distinction of various types of possibility, see *ibid.*, § 140, p. 292.
20. *Ibid.*, § 45, p. 84. Aron Gurwitsch, "La Philosophie phénoménologique en Allemagne," *Revue de métaphysique et de morale,* XXXV, no. 4 (1928), illuminates very well the role of *potentiality* in Husserlian idealism.

ment always indicate further aspects, and so on. Things are never known in their totality; an essential character of our perception of them is that of being inadequate.[21]

A material thing refers to a double relativity. On the one hand, a thing is relative to consciousness—to say that it exists is to say that it meets consciousness.[22] On the other hand, since the sequence of subjective phenomena is never completed, existence remains relative to the degree of completion of the sequence of "phenomena," and further experience may, in principle, falsify and reduce to a hallucination what had seemed to be acquired by a preceding perception.[23]

This characterization of the existence of material things is meant by Husserl to be only temporary, so its definitive elaboration is one of the main problems of phenomenology.[24] Yet it allows us to understand how, as Husserl says, "the existence of *transcendent objects* [25] is purely phenomenal," [26] how "the existence of a thing is never necessarily required by its mode of being given but is always in a certain way contingent," [27] and also how "all that is given of a thing in person could also not exist." [28] Finally, it allows us to understand Husserl's assertion concerning "the dubitable character of transcendent perception." [29]

It is obvious that this thesis does not assert that there is something doubtful about the perception of the world and that it is not opposed to the naïve and natural attitude of the man who lives in the existing world. *It is not a skeptical thesis.* It does not deny the value of external perception [30] by asserting its illusory character, its inadequation to genuine being. Such a skeptical thesis would not express a specifically philosophical attitude. While taking a stand opposite to that of the naïve attitude, it would still leave us on the same level as that of naïve life, since

21. See *Ideen,* § 3, p. 10; § 44, pp. 80–81; § 138, pp. 286–87; and *passim.*
22. *Ibid.,* § 50, pp. 93 f.
23. *Ibid.,* § 46, p. 86; § 138, p. 287.
24. *Ibid.,* § 55, pp. 107–8; § 96, p. 201.
25. The term *transcendent* means, for Husserl, everything which is not a constitutive part of the flux of consciousness (*ibid.,* § 38, p. 68). Hence, it means mainly material objects.
26. *Ibid.,* § 44, p. 80.
27. *Ibid.,* § 46, p. 86.
28. *Ibid.*
29. *Ibid.,* p. 85.
30. See *ibid.,* § 32, pp. 56–57; and especially § 55, p. 107.

then philosophy would merely deny everything which is asserted in the natural attitude. We would be discussing the existence or the nonexistence of the world, but we would still presuppose an unclarified concept of existence. We would fail to question this concept or we would rely implicitly on a pretheoretical noncritical concept of existence.

The novelty of the analyses which we have just described is precisely that, instead of making assertions about the certain or uncertain existence of things, they are asserting theses concerning *the very mode of existence of external things,* and this puts the problem on a new level. We could formulate the result of our analyses in the following way: the existence of material things contains in itself a nothingness, a possibility of not-being. This does not mean that things do not exist but that their mode of existing contains precisely the possible negation of itself.[31] This negation is not merely a characteristic of knowledge, as if we were only saying that knowledge of the physical world can never posit with certainty the existence of the world. Instead, one must take this possible negation as a constitutive element of the very existence of things.[32]

To avoid any misunderstanding, we must add that the contingency of material things that we assert here should not be taken to mean that existence is not included in the essence of material things, as it is in the essence of God, according to the famous ontological argument. The negation or contingency, which is inherent in existence, expresses no more than the duality of how external things reveal themselves and exist. This duality consists in the facts that a being is intimated, but it is intimated in an infinite sequence of subjective phenomena; that the existence of things is assimilated to the concordance of those phenomena, but this concordance is not necessary; hence, the claim of things to exist is relative to those phenomena which, at any moment, may become discordant. *Contingency, here, is not a relation between the essence and the existence of an object but a determination of the existence itself.* The purely phenomenal character of the existence of external things which Kant determines by opposition to the "things in themselves" appears here as an internal determination of this existence.

31. *Ibid.,* § 46, p. 87; § 49, p. 91; § 138, pp. 286–87.
32. *Ibid.,* § 44, p. 80. The mode of perception of a thing depends on the thing's "specific meaning."

Furthermore, if *contingency* had to be understood here by opposition to the necessity of the ontological argument, then the necessity of the existence of consciousness, which we shall study presently and which is opposed to the contingency of the physical world in Husserl's philosophy, would have to be understood in the sense of the ontological argument. But Husserl denies this explicitly.[33]

Nothing is granted to the skeptics. On the contrary, the origin and the true reasons for the mistakes of skepticism are explained. In the relative character of the existence of material things we find the foundation of skepticism. Skepticism created a chasm by hypostatizing as *being in itself* the claim of the subjective phenomena, to existence, while calling *knowledge* these same subjective phenomena, in the flux of their becoming. Noticing that the intimated thing is, in principle, inadequate to the phenomena which constitute it, skepticism seems to find the right to assert that we do not know being and that we are constantly misled by our senses. But skepticism is precisely so called because it does not recognize the value of being to what we know and is guided by an idea of being which expresses the existence of things in only one way, the way in which things claim to transcend the phenomena which constitute them. The great interest of Husserl's conception then seems to be his starting point (the phenomenological starting point *par excellence*): to have tried to locate the existence of external things, not in their opposition to what they are for consciousness, but in the aspect under which they are present in concrete conscious life. What exists for us, what we consider as existing is not a reality hidden behind phenomena that appear as images or signs of this reality.[34] The world of phenomena itself makes up the being of our concrete life. It is a world of phenomena that have no clearly defined limits and are not mathematically precise; they are full of "almost" and "so to speak," obeying the vague laws that are expressed by the word "normality." [35]

We can perceive how, with such an attitude, one can go beyond any philosophy which thinks it must start from the theory of knowledge, as a study of our faculty of knowing, in order to see whether and how a subject can reach being. Any theory of

33. *Ibid.*, § 46, pp. 86–87.
34. *Ibid.*, § 43, pp. 78–79.
35. This notion of normality is introduced in *ibid.*, § 44, pp. 81–82.

knowledge presupposes, indeed, the existence of an object and of a subject that must come in contact with each other. Knowledge is then defined as this contact, and this always leaves the problem of determining whether knowledge does not falsify the being which it presents to the subject. But this problem is exposed as fictitious once we understand that the origin of the very idea of "an object" is to be found in the concrete life of a subject; that a subject is not a substance in need of a bridge, namely, knowledge, in order to reach an object, but that the secret of its subjectivity is its being present in front of objects. The modes of appearing of things are not, therefore, characters which are superimposed on existing things by the process of consciousness; they make up the very existence of things.

Until now, however, we have proceeded negatively. We have shown that existence does not necessarily mean existence in the manner of things and that the existence of things in some way refers back to the existence of consciousness. What meaning does the being of consciousness have? How can it be positively determined? We must clarify these matters in order to reach the very heart of Husserl's ontology.

The fundamental intuition of Husserlian philosophy consists of attributing absolute existence to concrete conscious life and transforming the very notion of conscious life. This conscious life, which has an absolute existence, cannot be the same as what is meant by consciousness in Berkeleian idealism, a sort of closed world which has in fact the same type of existence as that of things. Conscious life must be described as life in the presence of transcendent beings. It must be understood that when we speak of the absolute existence of consciousness, when we assert that the external world is solely constituted by consciousness, we do not fall back into Berkeleianism; rather, we are going back to a more original phenomenon of existence that alone makes possible the subject and object of traditional philosophy. Those two terms are only abstractions based on the concrete phenomenon which is expressed by the Husserlian concept of consciousness.

We shall first describe the absolute character of the existence of consciousness and then show [36] how this existence consists in being intentional. It will then follow that consciousness is the origin of all being and that the latter is determined by the in-

36. See below, chap. 3.

trinsic meaning of the former. Thus we shall be in a position to understand how the study of conscious life, when understood in a certain way, may have a philosophical value.[37]

To determine the essence of consciousness, Husserl starts from the totality of those phenomena which are included in the Cartesian *cogito*.

> We are taking as a starting point "consciousness" in the pregnant sense of the term, in the sense which first comes to mind and which can be most easily expressed as the Cartesian *cogito,* as "I think." As we know, Descartes understood the *cogito* in a wide sense, in such a way as to include any state such as: "I perceive, I remember, I imagine, I judge, I desire, I want" and, similarly, all analogous ego states [*Icherlebnisse*] in their innumerable successive formations.[38]

Those states of life, those *Erlebnisse,* do not form a region of reality which is simply beside the world of nature.[39] It is only in terms of "empty categories"[40] that we may use the word "being" with respect to both the world of things and the world of consciousness. The *Erlebnisse* have a different mode of existence. We insist on this from the beginning. "Consciousness has in itself its proper being. . . . It constitutes *a region of being original in principle.*"[41] Elsewhere, Husserl says, even more explicitly, "There emerges an essential and fundamental difference between *being qua consciousness* and *being qua thing.*"[42] "In this way is intimated a difference in principle between the *modes of existence* of consciousness and of reality, the most important difference that there is."[43]

If we concentrate on the manner in which consciousness is revealed to reflective insight, we shall notice that, in the perception of consciousness or reflection (*immanent* perception, in Husserl's terminology), there is no duality between what is revealed and what is only intimated, as in external, transcendent percep-

37. See below, chap. 7.
38. *Ideen,* § 34, pp. 60–61. See also § 28, p. 50. The concept of consciousness here does not yet include the potential sphere. This is why Husserl speaks of consciousness "in the pregnant sense of the term."
39. *Ibid.,* § 39, p. 70; § 49, p. 93.
40. *Ibid.,* § 49, p. 93; § 76, p. 141.
41. *Ibid.,* § 33, p. 59 (my italics).
42. *Ibid.,* § 42, p. 76.
43. *Ibid.,* p. 77 (my italics); see also § 35, p. 62.

tion.[44] "Ein Erlebnis schattet sich nicht ab."[45] "For any being in this region it is nonsense to speak of appearance [*erscheinen*] or of representation by *Abschattungen*."[46]

> Psychical being, being as "phenomenon," is in principle not a unity that could be experienced in several separate perceptions as individually identical, not even in perceptions of the same subject. In the psychical sphere there is, in other words, no distinction between appearance and being, and if nature is a being that appears in appearances, still appearances themselves (which the psychologist certainly looks upon as psychical) do not constitute a being which itself appears by means of appearances lying behind it.[47]

The flux of consciousness is always given in immanent perception as something absolute, something which is what it is, and not as an object which is anticipated on the basis of a sequence of phenomena which may further contradict or destroy one another and consequently disappoint our expectations. Unlike the perception of external things, immanent perception is adequate.

> The perception of an *Erlebnis* is a direct vision [*schlichtes Erschauen*] of something which is given (or could be given) . . . in perception as something absolute and not as that which is identical in many *Abschattungen*. . . . A feeling does not appear through *Abschattungen*. Whenever I consider it I have . . . something absolute which has no sides that could be presented once in one way, once in another.[48]

That they may always turn out to be nothing is a characteristic of the existence of material things and is alien to a being which is revealed directly rather than in a sequence of *Abschattungen*. "In this absolute sphere . . . there is no room for discordance[49] or mere appearance, or for the possibility of being

44. For this terminology, see *ibid.*, § 38, p. 68.
45. *Ibid.*, § 42, p. 77; § 44, p. 81.
46. *Ibid.*, and § 49, p. 93.
47. *Phil. als str. Wiss.*, p. 312 [p. 106].
48. *Ideen*, § 44, p. 81.
49. *Discordance* may take place between successive phenomena which constitute the appearance of a material thing: the sequence of phenomena which intimate a "man" may be contradicted by the rest of the experience, which shows that it was a tree taken to be a man. This possibility—that the perceived object is, in truth, *something else* (that, in our example, the man is actually a tree)—is essentially inherent in the way external things appear.

something else.[50] It is a sphere of absolute position." [51] The analysis of immanent perception leads us to the absolute position of consciousness, to the impossibility of denying its existence.

> When reflective perception is directed toward my *Erlebnis*, what is perceived is an absolute *self* [*absolutes Selbst*], the existence of which cannot, in principle, be denied; that is, it is in principle impossible to suppose that it does not exist. To say of an *Erlebnis* given in such a way that it does not exist would be nonsense.[52]

We seem to be in the presence of the Cartesian *cogito;* there is no doubt about the relationship between the two ideas, and Husserl realizes it.

We shall return to the connections that can be found between Husserl's attitude and that of the Cartesian *cogito*, but let us say now that by stretching the connection too far, one could distort the most original thought of the German philosopher. Indeed, for Husserl, the absoluteness of consciousness means more than the indubitability of internal perception. This absoluteness does not concern only the truths pertaining to consciousness and their certainty but also the very existence of consciousness itself. To posit as absolute the existence of consciousness means more than the fact that it is absurd to doubt it.

It is important to show that Husserl has done more than render comprehensible the absolute evidence of the *cogito* by appealing to the fact that internal perception is adequate. For Husserl, it is the absoluteness of consciousness itself which makes possible an adequate perception. The absolute evidence of the *cogito* is founded on the mode of being of consciousness. "Only for the ego, and for the flux of experience in its relation to itself, do we find this exceptional situation; only here there is, and there must be, something like immanent perception." [53]

It is not only as object of reflection that consciousness, being given adequately, necessarily exists; the meaning of its existence consists precisely in not existing as an object of reflection only.

---

50. See preceding note.
51. *Ideen*, § 46, p. 86.
52. *Ibid.*, p. 85.
53. *Ibid.*, pp. 85–86. See also, in § 45, p. 83, an expression such as "zur Seinsart der Erlebnisses gehört es etc." Similarly, § 79, p. 157: "Jede Seinsart . . . hat wesensmässig ihre Gegebenheitsweisen." See also *ibid.*, § 111, p. 225.

Conscious life exists even when it is not an object of reflection. "What is perceived in it [in reflection] is precisely characterized as not having existence and duration in perception only, but as having been already there before becoming object of perception." [54] Here, the existence of consciousness reveals its independence with respect to internal perception, as opposed to external objects, whose very existence refers us back to consciousness.[55] It is no longer a reflection on consciousness that constitutes its existence; the former is made possible by the latter.

Furthermore, we have wondered whether the assertion that consciousness has an absolute existence remains, for Husserl, a mere thesis that he does not attempt to clarify. Indeed, we cannot say that the clarification of the meaning of this absoluteness has ever been attempted explicitly by Husserl. This is certainly one of the most serious gaps in his theory. He will study the notion of existence proper to the various regions of being; but, in the case of consciousness, back to which all regions refer, he will assert only its absolute existence.[56] And yet it seems to us that there is at least the beginning of an analysis which goes in that direction. Husserl characterizes the existence of consciousness and its independence from reflection by saying that consciousness "is ready to be perceived [*Wahrnehmungsbereit*]." [57] But for external objects, according to their mode of existing, to be ready to be perceived always means to be already in some way an object of consciousness—if only implicitly, as a part of the horizon of an actual perception.[58] Consciousness, on the other hand, is ready to be perceived in a quite different manner. For consciousness, to be perceivable does not mean to be already an object of consciousness but, more precisely, to exist in this special manner which is opposed to the mode of presence of objects to subjects. Consciousness is ready to be perceived "through the simple modality of its existence . . . for the ego to which it belongs." [59] This possibility of being perceived, a possibility which is inherent in the very existence of consciousness, derives, according to another text, from the fact that "all *Erlebnisse* are

---

54. *Ibid.*, § 45, p. 83.
55. *Ibid.*, § 38, p. 68. Concerning the notions of "dependent" and "independent," see below, pp. 109 ff.
56. See below, especially chap. 7.
57. *Ideen*, § 45, p. 84.
58. See above, pp. 21–22.
59. *Ideen*, § 45, p. 84.

conscious." [60] *Erlebnisse* are conscious. They know themselves in some manner, but this consciousness is not analogous to the perception of external objects or even to the immanent perception of reflection. Indeed, we also learn, and we can only make a note of it, that the existence of those experiences is equivalent to their being "constituted in the immanent consciousness of time." [61] "The consciousness . . . of time functions as perceptive consciousness." [62] But Husserl adds:

> This universal [*allumfassende*] consciousness of time is obviously not a continuous perception, in the pregnant sense of the term. . . . In other words, it is obviously not a continuous internal reflection for which *Erlebnisse* would be objects, *posited* in the specific meaning of the term and apprehended as existing. [63]

The specific mode of existence of consciousness—its absoluteness and its independence from reflection—consists in its existing for itself, prior to being taken in any way as an object by reflection. Consciousness exists in such a way that it is constantly present to itself.

> All real *Erlebnisse, qua* existing and present, or, as we could also say, *qua* temporal unity constituted in the phenomenological consciousness of time, carry in some sense, in themselves, their character of being *in a way analogous to perceived objects.* [64]

But that the "existence of *Erlebnisse*" [65] is in principle conscious does not mean that conscious life exists and then becomes conscious of itself. "It is certainly an absurdity to speak of a content of which we are 'unconscious,' one of which we are conscious only later." [66] Consciousness constitutes the very being of *Erlebnisse.* From this we understand the great importance of the phenomenological investigations on the constitution of immanent time.

To summarize: consciousness presents itself as a sphere of absolute existence. This absolute existence not only expresses the indubitable character of the *cogito* but also, *qua* positive

60. *Ibid.*, p. 83.
61. *Ibid.*, § 113, p. 229.
62. *Ibid.*
63. *Ibid.*
64. *Ibid.*; see also § 114, p. 235; § 118, pp. 245–46.
65. *Ibid.*, § 45, p. 85.
66. *Zeitbewusstsein*, p. 472 [p. 162].

determination of the very being of consciousness, founds the possibility of an indubitable *cogito.*

It is in this, we believe, that Husserl's conception of the *cogito* differs from Descartes's. For Descartes, indeed, the distinction between thought and space is, above all, a distinction between two types of knowledge, one absolutely certain, the other doubtful. There may be many reasons in favor of the truths that I can formulate, but they are never incontrovertible because, by its very nature, our sensibility is subject to error. The analysis of sensibility by Descartes exposes as relative and fallible what we assert on the basis of our senses. This analysis, however, is not presented as an analysis of the being of sensible things, but as an analysis of knowledge, that is, of the channels that put a subject in contact with being.

From among those doubtful truths there is, for Descartes, one that is privileged, namely, the *cogito;* but it is only one privileged piece of knowledge among others, a sort of axiom from which all the others should be deduced. "The soul is easier to know than the body." Because of the force of its certainty, knowledge of the soul is superior to knowledge of the body. One can then understand that, after the *cogito,* Descartes intends to deduce from the existence of consciousness that of God and of the external world. Descartes does not go back to the source of the evidence of the *cogito;* he does not search for its root in the being of consciousness which renders this evidence possible. For him, the meaning of existence is not a problem. He is probably led by the idea that to exist means always and everywhere the same thing, and he then simply wants to show that the external world exists just as he has shown that consciousness exists. For Husserl, the necessary existence of consciousness does not follow from the *cogito;* rather, this necessary existence is none other than an existence that allows a *cogito.* The *cogito* is not merely a means to attain a first certainty so as to deduce the existence of the world outside the *cogito.* What is interesting is the mode of existence of the *cogito,* the type of original existence that characterizes it. Hence Descartes is still on the grounds of dogmatic philosophy, if we call "dogmatic" a philosophy that begins with an unclarified idea of existence borrowed from the existence of hypostatized external things and then applies this type of existence to all the regions of being. For such a philosophy, the question is not to know what it is to be, but to know whether such and such an object exists. Against such a theory, skepticism has an easy task when it reduces the totality of being to appearance: if we admit that to exist is to exist in the manner of things, then we are forced to admit that such an existence is always problematic. Of course, the novelty of Cartesian philosophy consists in wanting to go beyond skepticism by abandoning the idea of existence conceived on the model of external things. If what appears does not exist, we are at least certain that the act of appearing exists. But Descartes did not follow his discovery to the end. Once he had reached, in consciousness, a domain of absolute existence, he did not see that the term "existence" is used there with a quite different meaning from the one it has when applied to the world of spatial things. He interpreted the former on the model of the latter. The soul, for Descartes, is a substance which has an existence parallel to that of extended substances and is distinguished from them solely by the certainty we have of its existence. The specific character of the *cogito* is not understood by Descartes as the internal character of the substantiality of consciousness.

This is where Husserl has made progress. The evidence of the *cogito* is grounded on the mode of existence of consciousness in the same way that appearing characterizes the very being of external things. The difference between those two modes of knowing is not limited to their degree of certainty: it is a difference in nature. An abyss separates the adequation of internal perception and the non-adequation of external perception. Husserl's step forward beyond Descartes consists in not separating the knowledge of an object—or, more generally, the mode of appearing of an object in our life—from its being; it consists of seeing the mode of its being known as the expression and the characteristic of its mode of being. This is why, in Husserl's philosophy, there is for the first time a possibility of passing from and through the theory of knowledge to the theory of being. The latter will consist of directly studying the essence of beings that are revealed to consciousness, and of studying the modes of existence in the different regions of objects. Let us say, incidentally, that with the idea of a different existence for external things and for consciousness, there arises the very possibility of different modes of existence. We shall return to this in the last part of this work.

We have tried to characterize the absolute existence of consciousness by indicating the conscious character of *Erlebnisse*, the character by virtue of which they are always present to themselves. This absolute existence should not be understood as it would be in an "ontological argument."

Husserl explicitly states that, for him, the existence of consciousness is simply factual. "Clearly, the necessity of the existence of each actual *Erlebnis* is not a pure essential necessity, i.e., a pure eidetic [67] particularization of an eidetic law. It is a factual necessity." [68] The *Seinsnotwendigkeit* of consciousness must mean something quite different from an existence that follows necessarily from an essence. It concerns not the fact that consciousness exists but the mode of its existence. It does not mean that consciousness necessarily exists but that inasmuch as it exists its existence does not contain the possibility of its not-being which is the characteristic of spatial existence. *To exist*, in the case of consciousness, does not mean *to be perceived* in a series of subjective phenomena, but *to be* continuously present to itself, which is what the term "consciousness" expresses.

Now we can understand how Husserl could meet the objection raised by Hering in *Phénoménologie et philosophie religieuse*. Hering's objection concerns the impossibility of passing from the indubitability of the *cogito* to the assertion of its necessary existence. "Indeed," says Hering,

> in this case the fact in question derives its indubitability not from the idea of the *cogito* (as is the case for the ideal existence of an essence or in the case of the actual existence of God for the ontologists) but from the particularly favorable situation of the observer. So Paul could perfectly well imagine a world in which the consciousness of Pierre would not exist.[69]

Hering is perfectly right in saying that the existence of the *cogito* does not have the same meaning as "the existence of God for the ontologists," since, as we have tried to show, Husserl himself admits this. However, if the necessity of consciousness is, according to our interpretation, a characteristic of the mode and not of the fact of its existence, one can no longer appeal to its privileged situation which allows it to reflect upon itself, in order to dispute the necessary character of the existence of consciousness. The possibility of such a *privileged situation* is precisely what characterizes the existence of consciousness. In

67. Concerning this term, see below, p. 104.
68. *Ideen*, § 46, p. 86.
69. Jean Hering, *Phénoménologie et philosophie religieuse* (Paris: Alcan, 1925), p. 85.

the being of consciousness is founded the very possibility of reflection. "Only for the ego and for the flux of experience in its relation to itself, do we find this exceptional situation; only here there is, and there must be, something like immanent perception." [70]

The analyses of the existence which is proper to external things and to consciousness have not shown, as a superficial reading of Husserl's works could lead one to believe, that only consciousness exists and that the external world does not. Both exist, but according to two different modes.

However, we must now emphasize a certain primacy of consciousness which is crucial for the whole of Husserl's philosophy and which, above all, is vital for understanding the function and the place of intuition in his system. Consciousness exists absolutely; this is guaranteed by every moment of its existence. [71] But to say that consciousness, in the concrete totality of its course, carries with it the guarantee of its being amounts to saying that existence should not be looked for somewhere behind it, but that, with all the wealth of its details and meanderings, it is itself being, and that it is here that the notion of existence must be sought. Husserl's assertion in § 49 of *Ideen* that consciousness "nulla re indiget ad existendum" does not, we believe, mean anything else. It is in this primacy of conscious life that naturalism is definitively superseded. Its last objection against that for which the intrinsic meaning of our conscious life bears witness could consist, as we have shown, in presenting all that life means as a purely subjective phenomenon incapable of saying anything about *being*. We have tried to establish that the norm of being used by naturalism does not apply to all beings, and that consciousness exists in a different way. Furthermore, our analyses have shown that the existence of consciousness is absolute and that consciousness carries in itself the guarantee of its being, while the being of naturalism returns back to consciousness, which it presupposes as its source. Only consciousness can make intelligible to us the meaning of the being of the world which is a certain mode of meeting consciousness or of appearing to it. [72] The world of nature, from which naturalism derives its notion of existence, only exists itself in

70. *Ideen*, § 46, pp. 85–86.
71. *Ibid.*, p. 85.
72. *Ibid.*, § 76, p. 141.

the measure in which it enters the life of consciousness.[73] But, precisely because concrete life contains in different manners different regions of objects, *to be* does not mean the same thing for each of those regions. Their proper mode of being met by, or constituted for, consciousness must become the object of philosophy, and, as we shall see, it must, according to Husserl, constitute philosophy's central problem.[74]

However, by presenting the idea of a sphere which is the origin of all beings and prompts us to transform the very concept of being, seeing it no longer as the idea of substance but as that of subjectivity, do we not fall back into a form of Berkeleian idealism where to be contained in consciousness is the total measure of reality?

It is clear enough from our previous considerations that we are not dealing here with an idealism for which the assertion of the purely phenomenal existence of the external world means a devaluation of it. The external world exists, it is what it is, and to see it as being only a phenomenon is to clarify the sense of its existence; it is to show, after having looked at the life in which it is given, what its mode of occurring in life is.[75]

There is another matter which separates Husserlian idealism from that of someone like Berkeley. For Husserl, it is not a matter of reducing the world of spatial objects to contents of consciousness,[76] and in fact of attributing to these contents the mode of existence of the material objects which have been drowned in them. On the contrary, the point is to show—and we have indefatigably emphasized it—that the sphere to which all existence refers back has a specific manner of existing. This specific existence lets us surmise that we are not in the presence here of a subject opposed to an object, of a being which is antithetical to objects and, for that reason, is precisely on the same level as them. For Husserl, consciousness is a primary domain which alone renders possible and comprehensible an "object" and a "subject," terms that are already derivative.

It is in this last point, which is the object of the following chapter, that the main difference between Husserl and Berkeleian idealism lies. Consciousness for Husserl and consciousness for British empiricism (highly tainted with naturalism) have nothing

73. *Ibid.*, § 47, pp. 88–89.
74. See below, chap. 7 and Conclusion.
75. *Ideen*, § 55, p. 107.
76. *Ibid.*, § 98, p. 206.

in common but the name. So far we have characterized the existence of the absolute sphere of life as *consciousness*, i.e., as existing by being, prior to any reflection, present to itself. But we still must establish a characteristic of the other structural elements of consciousness, which are as important as the first.

3 / The Phenomenological Theory of Being: The Intentionality of Consciousness

CONSCIOUSNESS, whose existence we have established in the preceding chapter, is a temporal flow.[1] Conscious life takes place in *immanent time,* which is very different from cosmic time, from the time of nature.[2] The constitution of consciousness in time, the structure of time itself, the internal consciousness of time, and the historicity which thus characterizes consciousness, are subjects which have much preoccupied Husserl in the course of his phenomenological investigations.[3] Their examination has a great deal to contribute to the clarification of the fact which we have expressed by saying: "All *Erlebnisse* are conscious."[4]

However, here, where we are mainly concerned with intuition, we must abstract from the constitution of immanent time and consider consciousness as being already constituted in time.[5] A characteristic aspect of the existence of consciousness as it is then given to us is intentionality: the fact that all consciousness is not only consciousness but also consciousness of something, i.e., related to an object. We shall begin with a more general concept of "experience" (*Erlebnis*) which, at first, may seem at least unrelated to intentionality.

1. *Ideen,* § 81, p. 163.
2. *Ibid.,* p. 161; *Zeitbewusstsein,* p. 369 [p. 23].
3. *Ideen,* § 81, pp. 161–65; and *Zeitbewusstsein.*
4. *Ideen,* § 113, p. 229.
5. Husserl allows this, in *ibid.,* § 118, pp. 245–46.

By *Erlebnis,* in a wide sense, we understand everything which takes place in the flow of consciousness, and consequently, not only intentional *Erlebnisse,* actual or potential cogitations . . . but everything that is real in the flow of consciousness and in its concrete parts. . . . Not every real element constitutive of the concrete unity of an intentional *Erlebnis* is itself intentional, i.e., has the property of being *consciousness of something.* This is true for example of all the sense-data [*Empfindungsdaten*] which play such an important role in the perceptive intuition of a thing.[6]

In another passage, some examples make clearer what we must understand by *sensation.* They are

data of color, sound, and tactile feeling, etc., and must not be con- fused with such elements of things as color, roughness, etc. which are represented in conscious life through these data. They are also the sensuous impressions of pleasure, pain, tickle, etc. and the sensuous *moments* in the sphere of impulses.[7]

We learn, moreover, that those elements which are deprived of intentionality constitute a special material or *hyletic* level which is the object of a phenomenological discipline, the *hyletic* dis- cipline, which describes the structure of that level.[8]

We must therefore deal with sensations (or with phantasms,[9] in the case of imagination) which have a striking similarity to those simple elements by means of which empiricists' psychology meant to reconstruct our internal life. However, there is a great difference between the two. Let us begin by paying special atten- tion to the following passage in the above quotation: "data . . . [which] must not be confused with such elements of things as color, roughness, etc., which are represented in conscious life through these data." As Husserl himself says elsewhere,[10] the hyletic data to which the qualitative moments of things corre- spond are deeply different from them. Only by denying this would Husserl go back to the sensualist conception of consciousness and deny intentionality or, at least, go back to the distinction be- tween real objects and the mental images which are their reflec- tion in consciousness. However, objects are not collections of

6. *Ibid.,* § 36, p. 65; see also § 41, p. 75.
7. *Ibid.,* § 85, p. 172.
8. *Ibid.,* p. 173; § 86, p. 178.
9. Concerning the relation between phantasms and sensations, see *ibid.,* § 112, p. 227; *Zeitbewusstsein,* pp. 405, 441 [pp. 69, 115].
10. *LU,* II, 348–49 [p. 537]; *Ideen,* § 81, p. 162; § 97, p. 202.

"sensations." It would be mistaken to believe that new characters superimposed on "sensations," or a new viewpoint on these contents of conscious life, could transform them into "external objects." There is a difference of nature between red as a subjective and experienced sensation and red as objective and represented.[11]

> The sense-data which function as *Abschattungen* of color, gloss, or shape must be distinguished from color, gloss, and shape themselves, i.e., from any "moment" of things. An *Abschattung*, although it bears the same name, is in principle of a different type than what it represents. An *Abschattung* is an experience. But an experience is possible only as an experience and not as anything spatial. But, what is given in an *Abschattung* can, in principle, only be spatial (such is its essence) and cannot be an experience.[12]

To oppose the hyletic data to the sensations of the sensualists, we must still emphasize that the character which gives unity to those contents which are grouped under the concept of *hyle* is not the purely extrinsic character of being provided by the senses. This was sufficient for empiricism. But for us this unity proceeds from an internal character [13] which permits us to extend the notion of *hyle* beyond sense-data to the sphere of affectivity and of will.[14] The flow of consciousness, however, does not consist only of the hyletic level.

We can distinguish in consciousness an animating act which gives to the hyletic phenomena a transcendent meaning: [15] they signify something from the external world, they represent it, desire it, love it, etc. This act is an element which has a mode of existing identical to that of hyletic data, i.e., it is conscious and constituted in immanent time; it knows itself in the implicit manner which is characteristic of *Erlebnisse*.[16] Yet it gives a meaning to the flow of consciousness.[17] It intends something other than itself; it transcends itself.

The object toward which consciousness tends when it transcends itself in an intention is not a real element, a content of

---

11. *Zeitbewusstsein*, p. 371 [p. 25].
12. *Ideen*, § 41, pp. 75–76.
13. *Ibid.*, § 85, p. 173.
14. *Ibid.*
15. *Ibid.*, pp. 172–73.
16. *Ibid.*, § 113, p. 229.
17. *Ibid.*, § 85, p. 174.

consciousness, as would be assumed in a Berkeleian idealism. A Berkeleian idealism does not distinguish between qualities of objects and hyletic data, and it treats the transcendence of objects with respect to consciousness as a mere subjective appearance. *Intentionality is, for Husserl, a genuine act of transcendence and the very prototype of any transcendence.* This introduces us to the study of intentionality, which we shall complete in detail because it is as important a character of the existence of *Erlebnisse* as the fact that they are conscious. "It is intentionality which characterizes consciousness in the pregnant sense of the term, and which at the same time allows for the characterization of the whole flow of experience as a conscious flow and as the unity of one consciousness." [18]

The term *intention* must be taken in a larger sense than the one it has in expressions such as "good intention" or "having the intention of doing this or that." It expresses the fact, which at first does not seem original,[19] that each act of consciousness is conscious of something: each perception is the perception of a perceived object, each desire the desire of a desired object, each judgment the judgment of a "state of affairs" (*Sachverhalt*) about which one makes a pronouncement, etc.[20] But we shall soon realize the philosophical interest of this property of consciousness and the profound transformation that it brings to the very notion of consciousness.

In order to make more precise the notion of intentionality, Husserl says in the *Logische Untersuchungen:*

> If this experience is present, then, *eo ipso* and through its own essence (we must insist), the intentional "relation" to an object is achieved, and an object is "intentionally present"; the two phrases mean precisely the same.[21]

There is here a primary and irreducible notion which may seem irrational in view of the naturalist conception of being, an inert being to which it would be absurd to apply the category of "self-transcendence." This remark is directed precisely against psychologistic naturalism. Intentionality in Husserl cannot be taken as a *property* of consciousness, i.e., as a character which is unrelated to the mode of existing of consciousness, as simply a

18. *Ibid.*, § 84, p. 168.
19. *Ibid.*, § 96, p. 200.
20. *Ibid.*, § 84, p. 168.
21. *LU*, II, 372–73 [p. 558].

modality of the contents of consciousness. It is precisely the very mode of existence of consciousness that the notion of intentionality tries to characterize.[22]

But Husserl also attacks a theory which would see in intentionality a new element, a bridge between the world and consciousness. When one speaks of intentionality, the question is not "the connection between some psychological event named 'experience' and another real being named 'object'; nor is it a psychophysical . . . relation between the two which takes place in objective reality." [23] In this hypothesis, intentionality would be a means of explaining the way consciousness relates to the world, a way of answering the question: "How does a subject reach a transcendent object?" In this case, unless one saw in intentionality a purely verbal solution, to speak of intentionality would amount to admitting that consciousness exists as a substance and that one of its attributes is its intentionality, which allows this substance, as subject, to enter into contact with another reality. However, intentionality is not the way in which a subject tries to make contact with an object that exists beside it. *Intentionality is what makes up the very subjectivity of subjects.* The very reality of subjects consists in their transcending themselves. The problem of the relation between subject and object was justified by a substantialist ontology which conceived existence on the model of things resting in themselves. Then, any relation to something alien was extremely mysterious. As we have shown, Husserl, by overcoming the substantialist concept of existence, was able to demonstrate that a subject is not something that first exists and then relates to objects. The relation between subjects and objects constitutes the genuinely primary phenomenon in which we can find what are called "subject" and "object." [24] The fact that Husserl has, from the

22. In Albert Spaier, *La Pensée concrète* (Paris: Alcan, 1927), where Spaier deals with the notion of intentionality in Husserl, the *ontological* meaning of intentionality is not noticed. We make this point because Spaier's work is one of the rare books in France discussing Husserl.

23. *Ideen*, § 36, p. 64.

24. The notion of being, determined by the intrinsic meaning of life, allows Husserl to go beyond the scholastic theory of mental objects according to which intentional objects are only a subjective image of real beings. If what is called *mental image* had in consciousness the meaning of "image of something else," we could speak of images. But perceived objects are presented as being per-

beginning, seen in intentionality the *substantiality* of consciousness is the probable reason for his opposition to the idea of the "ego" as substance of consciousness, an opposition which is very noticeable in the first edition of Volume II of the *Logische Untersuchungen*.[25] It must have seemed to him that the idea of the ego necessarily leads to seeing in intentionality nothing but an accident of this ego-substance. It is only in *Ideen* that Husserl has succeeded in reconciling the personal character of consciousness with intentionality.[26]

Therefore, far from adding one more verbal solution to an old problem, the idea of intentionality permits us to go beyond the problem of the relation between subjects and objects.[27]

The intentionality of consciousness is a thesis borrowed by Husserl from Brentano, who had remained, however, on an empiricist and naturalistic ground.[28] Brentano had obtained the thesis from scholastic philosophy. Scholasticists knew that, without adjudicating existence or nonexistence to an object of thought (this, because of their substantialist conception of being, creates a special problem), we can, while remaining inside the immanent sphere of consciousness, speak of a relation to objects, a relation which is an essential characteristic of consciousness. Scholasticists called this immanent object of consciousness the mental or intentional object.[29] No doubt mental objects were numerically distinct from the real objects of which the mental objects were only the images. This is why this conception of consciousness had not yet reached the originality of Husserl's conception. Consciousness was a sphere closed upon itself, and intentionality

---

ceived "in person" (*ibid.*, § 90, p. 186). In perception, we do not deal with the world of images that indicate something behind themselves, the way that a portrait, in essence, refers back to the existence of an original. In perception, we deal with the original itself. In fact, it is arbitrary to interpose a mental image between consciousness and the original; it is a pure hypothesis which is in no way revealed by internal intuition (*ibid.*, § 90, p. 186; *LU*, II, 421–25 [pp. 593–96]). Furthermore, mental images, given as realities *in* consciousness, must themselves be known. But they can only be known by means of new mental images, and so on *ad infinitum*, which is absurd (*Ideen*, § 90).

25. See *LU*, II, 375 [p. 560].
26. See the end of this chapter.
27. This question is treated again in detail below, chap. 7, p. 123.
28. *Ideen*, § 85, pp. 174–75.
29. *Ibid.*, § 90, pp. 185 f.

remained a phenomenon internal to it.[30] The intentional character of consciousness did not issue in a genuine but in a purely psychological transcendence. Conscious life remained, in its existence, a substance patterned after material things. Intentionality did not constitute its very mode of existing. What is interesting about the Husserlian conception is its having put contact with the world at the very heart of the being of consciousness.

So far we have characterized intentionality as a relation to objects. This character does not affect only the purely theoretical life of the mind. In fact, all the forms of our life, affective, practical, and aesthetic, are characterized by a relation to an object.[31]

> Every valuation is a valuation of a *Wertverhalt* (state of value), every desire is a desire of a *Wunschverhalt*, etc. . . . Acting is directed at the action, love at what is loved, satisfaction at what is satisfying, etc.[32]

In each of these acts,

> our gaze is directed like a ray from the pure ego to the object correlated to the relevant state of consciousness (thing, state of things, etc.) and achieves *the consciousness of this object* which may be very different from case to case.[33]

The end of this quotation emphasizes an important point: "which may be very different from case to case." This means that intentionality is not an act which is always identical, which is present in all forms of consciousness, and which alone exercises the function of relating to an object, while specifically affective or voluntary coefficients, relegated to the rank of purely subjective phenomena, are added to an always identical intention. *Intentionality itself is different in each of these cases.* In each act the voluntary and affective elements are special ways of being directed toward an outside object, special ways of transcending oneself. Husserl states this explicitly elsewhere:

> The manner in which a mere representation refers to its object differs from the manner of a judgment which treats the same

30. *Ibid.*
31. *Ibid.*, § 117, p. 241.
32. *Ibid.*, § 84, p. 168.
33. *Ibid.*, p. 169.

state of affairs as true or false. Quite different again is the manner of a surmise or doubt, the manner of a hope or fear.[34]

Despite the precisions (and reservations) which we will have to add to these remarks in the next chapter, what we have just said is of primordial importance for understanding intentionality and the Husserlian spirit in general. We have shown that an experienced object has, through its very mode of being experienced, a right to being, and that conscious life is identical with the source of the idea of being. We see now that concrete life must be taken in all its forms and not merely in the theoretical form. Correlatively, the real world is not simply a world of things correlative to perceptive acts (purely theoretical acts); the real world is a world of objects of practical use and values.[35] The qualities that make things important to us (*Bedeutsamkeitsprädikate*) or dear to us, that make us fear them or want them, etc., are intrinsic characteristics which must not be excluded from the constitution of the world and must not be attributed solely to the "subjective reaction" of men that are in the world.[36] Since these characteristics are given in our life as correlates of intentions, they must be considered as belonging to the sphere of objectivity.[37] Let it be well understood: the fact that the attributes "valuable," "useful," or "being wanted" belong to the sphere of objectivity does not mean that they are given in a theoretical representation. It is precisely the very wide extension of the Husserlian notion of intentionality that makes it interesting. It expresses only the very general fact that consciousness transcends itself, that it directs itself toward something other than itself, that it has a sense.[38] But "to have a sense" does not mean the same as "to represent." [39] The act of love has a sense, but this does not mean that it includes a representation of the object loved together with a purely *subjective* [40] feeling which has no sense and which accompanies the representation. The characteristic of the loved object is precisely to be given in a love

34. *LU*, II, 367, and especially p. 368 [pp. 554–55].
35. *Ideen*, § 95, p. 198.
36. *Ibid.*, § 33, p. 58.
37. *Ibid.*, § 152, p. 318.
38. *Ibid.*, § 90, p. 185.
39. *Ibid.*, § 37, p. 66.
40. Spinoza's definition of love makes this mistake: "Amor nihil aliud est quam Laetitia concomitante idea causae externae," *Ethics* (The Hague: Nijhoff, 1882), XIII, 13.

intention, an intention which is irreducible to a purely theoretical representation.[41]

Value or affective predicates therefore belong to the existence of the world, which is not an "indifferent" medium of pure representations. The existence of a book, for instance, cannot be reduced to the simple fact of its being there, in front of us, as a set of physical properties. It is, rather, its practical and useful character which constitutes its existence; it is given to us in a manner quite different from a stone, for example. Concrete life, the source of the existence of the world, is not pure *theory*, although for Husserl the latter has a special status. It is a life of action and feeling, will and aesthetic judgment, interest and indifference, etc. It follows that the world which is correlative to this life is a sensed or wanted world, a world of action, beauty, ugliness, and meanness, as well as an object of theoretical contemplation. All these notions constitute in the same measure the existence of the world. *They constitute its ontological structures in the same measure as*, for instance, *the purely theoretical categories of spatiality.* This is one of the most interesting consequences of the Husserlian attitude. This is why, as we have often said and as we shall see in detail in our last chapter, the existence of the world is not an empty form that could be applied to all the domains of being. Will, desire, etc., are intentions which, along with representations, constitute the existence of the world. They are not elements of consciousness void of all relation to objects. Because of this, the existence of the world has a rich structure which differs in each different domain.

The preceding shows that intentionality is constitutive of *all* forms of consciousness. We have so far considered only explicit, awakened, or "active" consciousness, as Husserl calls it. But the field of conscious life is not limited to the full clarity and distinction in which each act is sharply articulated. Is the potential sphere also intentional? [42] Husserl answers affirmatively. Potential consciousness appears also as "consciousness of something"; [43] "the background of actual consciousness is neither a content of consciousness nor its matter; it is not void of intentionality, as are sensations which are given as present but per-

41. See Alexander Pfänder, "Zur Psychologie der Gesinnungen," in *Jahrbuch für Philosophie und phänomenologische Forschung*, Vols. I (1913) and III (1916).
42. See above, chap. 2.
43. *Ideen*, § 36, p. 64.

form no objective apprehension."[44] The background of consciousness is a sphere of objectivity. Differences in actuality and potentiality presuppose intentionality and are only its modalities.[45] Attention, according to Husserl's analyses, is not a distinct type of act, as perception is distinct from will, but is a possible mode of all acts. It neither transforms nor creates intentionality but is in some manner a "subjective modification" of it.[46] Within each type of intentionality, attention expresses the manner in which the ego relates to its object. In the act of attention the ego lives actively; it is in some manner spontaneous and free.[47] In acts void of attention, in the potential sphere, the ego is not directly busy with the given things. It is not actively and spontaneously directed toward objects.[48] Let us remark here that formulae such as "the ego lives spontaneously," "the ego is, or is not, busy with its object," have only a descriptive meaning which is already within the sphere of intentionality.[49]

In summary, both the potential *cogito* and the actual *cogito* are "consciousness of something." Intentionality appears as the very essence of consciousness.[50]

> The concept of intentionality, understood as we conceived it in this wide and indeterminate way, represents an indispensable primary and fundamental concept for the beginning of phenomenology. The general fact it denotes may be, prior to a closer scrutiny, extremely vague. It may occur in a vast number of essentially different contexts. It may be very difficult to cause its pure essence to appear through a rigorous and clear analysis, and to show which of the components of concrete contexts have this essence in them and which do not. Yet concrete life is thrown in a very interesting light when we recognize it as being intentional and when we say that it is consciousness of something.[51]

If there is, in the flow of consciousness, a hyletic level which is void of intentionality and must be animated by intentionality in order to receive a meaning and to intend an object outside of itself, are we not led back to a traditional conception of conscious-

44. *Ibid.*, § 84, p. 169.
45. *Ibid.*, pp. 169–70; § 92, p. 190.
46. *Ibid.*, §§ 92, 93, pp. 191 ff.; see § 93, p. 193n.
47. *Ibid.*, § 84, pp. 168–69; § 92, p. 192.
48. *Ibid.*
49. See below, p. 50.
50. *Ideen*, § 36, p. 64.
51. *Ibid.*, § 84, p. 171.

ness, considered as a substance resting in itself and having a mysterious relation to objects? Despite the contrary assertions which we have just quoted, does not intentionality play the role of a bridge that relates subjects and objects? Is it not Berkeleian idealism which reappears in this guise?

The spirit of Husserl's system, and the role played in it by the idea of intentionality, are clearly opposed to such a supposition.

First, the hyletic data, as is demonstrated by the Husserlian constitution of time, are already constituted by a deeper intentionality proper to consciousness, one from which we have abstracted in this study.[52] An *Empfindung* is something material only from the point of view of an already constituted flow,[53] but a sensation is comprehensible only as correlative to an act of sensation, an act which is deeper and has a very special structure. Therefore, intentionality is at the heart of consciousness. It is the first and last element of consciousness, which is no longer an object for anything else.

> We must . . . understand apprehension [*Auffassung*] [54] here in a twofold sense: as that which is immanently constituted, and as that which belongs to the immanent constitution, to the phases of the primordial flux itself, the primal apprehension which is no longer constituted.[55]

However, if the intentional character of consciousness is now beyond doubt; if internal intentionality, as an ultimate reality which is no longer constituted, creates its own existence; and, consequently, even if a sensualist thesis is excluded from Husserl's theory of sensation, our initial problem concerning the relation between consciousness and the world still remains. Is not the internal intentionality which forms the very character of consciousness self-sufficient? Does intentionality, when directed toward a transcendent object, constitute a new phenomenon in the realm of consciousness?

Husserl never stops repeating that intentionality is the very essence of consciousness.[56] However, in *Ideen* there is a passage

---

52. *Zeitbewusstsein*, p. 482 [pp. 176–77]; *Ideen*, § 81, pp. 162–63; § 85, p. 171.
53. *Zeitbewusstsein*, p. 482 [pp. 176–77].
54. This is another word for *intention*.
55. *Zeitbewusstsein*, p. 444 [p. 119].
56. *Ideen*, § 146, p. 303; § 84, p. 168; and *passim*.

which would suggest the opposite. When he elaborates the concepts of *hyle* and of the noetic form or intentionality which animates the *hyle*, Husserl leaves open the question of knowing whether "a matter without form or a form without matter" are possible.[57] It seems, therefore, that the separation of *hyle* and intentionality is considered at least conceivable. This text, however does not decide the matter.

Another passage of *Ideen* seems clearer. As a necessary complement to the analysis of the existence of consciousness, Husserl presents the hypothesis of the possible existence of a consciousness without a world, a consciousness reduced to pure immanence.[58] However, this is in the famous section of *Ideen* (§ 49) which led to so many reservations and so many accusations of idealism.[59] We agree with Hering's refusal to follow Husserl in that direction, but the ground on which we challenge Husserl's thesis is not so much his assertion that things have only a phenomenal existence, the assertion which is the main focus of Hering's reluctance. We do not believe that things should have an existence independent of consciousness, since their dependence, according to our interpretation, is not conceived as the negation of transcendent existence but as its characteristic. We do not believe that consciousness needs things in order to exist, although things need consciousness.[60] There we agree with Husserl. But if we follow Husserl on this last point, we find that our agreement is possible precisely because he does not conceive of consciousness at a level where it would make sense to speak of its dependence or independence with respect to the world. The precise function of intentionality is to characterize consciousness as a primary and original phenomenon, from which the subject and the object of traditional philosophy are only abstractions. In other words, it seems to us that if Husserlian idealism should not be followed, it is not because it is an idealism but because it is prejudiced against the mode of existence of consciousness as intentionality.

Moreover, one should not use §49 as a basic text, as Hering has already said. Inasmuch as one sees, in § 49, a negation of the fundamental role of intentionality, we can agree that it is

57. *Ibid.*, § 85, p. 172.
58. *Ibid.*, § 49, p. 92.
59. See Jean Hering, *Phénoménologie et philosophie religieuse* (Paris: Alcan, 1925), pp. 83 ff.
60. This is the opinion of Hering, *ibid.*, pp. 85–86.

in no way presupposed by all the other works of Husserl. One should probably even interpret § 49 on the basis of the whole system, taking the central role played in the system by intentionality into account. One could then note that the text of § 49 which asserts the possibility of a consciousness without a world [61] does not say explicitly that the flow of consciousness *may lack any transcendent intentionality.* At most, it shows that this flow may not constitute this being which we call "world" and which is a transcendent being with a well-determined structure. We are also prompted so to interpret this text by assertions like that in the passage below, which concludes another discussion of the hypothesis of the possible destruction of the world: "It does not change anything to the absolute existence of *Erlebnisse;* on the contrary, the latter are presupposed by it." [62] Does not this assertion, "[they] are presupposed by it," mean that the destruction of the world is a phenomenon that has a positive meaning and necessarily implies a consciousness which, consequently, would still have a transcendent meaning once the world had been destroyed, at least that of "destroyed world"?

Moreover, there is another text, earlier than the *Ideen* yet quite conclusive, in which Husserl explicitly asserts the impossibility of a consciousness without intentionality.

> The concept of "experience" has its prime source in the field of "psychic *acts.*" Even if this concept has been widened to include *non-acts,* these for us stand connected with, ranged beside and attached to *acts* in a unity of consciousness so essential that, were it to fall away, talk of "experiencing" would lose its point.[63]

In less explicit form, there are numerous similar assertions in *Ideen.*[64]

61. "Denn Vernichtung der Welt besagt korrelativ nichts anderes als dass in jedem Erlebnisstrom . . . gewisse geordnete Erfahrungszusammenhänge und demgemäss auch nach ihnen sich orientierenden Zusammenhänge theoretischer Vernunft ausgeschlossen wären. Darin liegt aber nicht, dass andere Erlebnisse und Erlebniszusammenhänge ausgeschlossen wären." It is true that these *Erlebniszusammenhänge* are not characterized in this text as being intentional, but they are not characterized at all.

62. *Ideen,* § 46, p. 87.

63. *LU,* II, 365n. [p. 553]. The notions of *act* and *non-act* which we have emphasized in this quotation are equivalent to those of intention and non-intention (*Ideen,* § 84, p. 170).

64. *Ideen,* § 84, p. 169; § 85, p. 171; § 86, p. 176; § 146, p. 303; and *passim.*

A description of the structure of consciousness and of intentionality cannot overlook the *personal* character of consciousness.
Psychic life is not an anonymous flow in time. Experiences always belong to an ego.[65] In the *Logische Untersuchungen*, Husserl denies that the ego is an element of the intentions. The ego
is identical with the totality of the intentions which fill a certain
time and which are mutually complementary. In *Ideen* some
progress is made, and the ego appears as an irreducible element
of conscious life.[66] Acts originate, so to speak, from the ego
which lives in these acts.[67] It is according to the mode in which it
lives in these acts that one distinguishes the receptivity from the
spontaneity of consciousness and from intentionality. The activity of the self when it is attentive, in acts of creative judgment and synthesis, of assertion and negation,[68] the spontaneity
of the self in all its forms, must be faithfully described before
being interpreted.[69] In some of these "positional" acts the self
lives, not as passively present in them but as a center of radia-
tion, "as the first source of their production." [70] There is in these
acts a sort of "fiat" of the self.

But though the ego is active and can be grasped in an actual
cogito, it is still not without relation to the potential sphere of
consciousness, precisely because it is, in a sense, turned away
from this sphere. This fact of being "turned away" positively
determines the potential sphere: it is potential because the ego
is turned away from it. The very possibility which is characteristic of the self, to turn away from this field and then to turn
itself toward it again, presupposes that this field belongs in
principle to the self. The background of consciousness belongs
to the *self* as his own; it is, so to speak, the field of its freedom.[71]

Husserl therefore reasserts the Kantian proposition that "*I
think* must accompany all my representations." [72]

In *Ideen* the ego remains an empty form, impossible to determine.[73] This conception has changed in the course of the evolution of Husserl's thought that forthcoming publications will make

65. *Ibid.*, § 80, pp. 159–60; § 81, p. 163; § 82, p. 165; and *passim*.
66. *Ibid.*, § 57, p. 109.
67. *Ibid.*, § 80, p. 160.
68. *Ibid.*, § 106, p. 219.
69. *Ibid.*, § 57, p. 110.
70. *Ibid.*, § 122, p. 253; § 92, p. 189; § 52, p. 102.
71. *Ibid.*, § 80, p. 160; § 57, p. 109; § 92, p. 192.
72. *Ibid.*, § 57, p. 109.
73. *Ibid.*, § 80, p. 160.

accessible to the public. In these studies Husserl considers the self in all its concrete aspects, giving the beginning of a phenomenological clarification to the old problems of personality, the nature of habitus, etc. In these studies, the ego is no longer reduced to an empty, purely formal point from which acts originate; it is considered as "personality." Before speaking more explicitly of this, we must wait for the publication of these works.

Here we are interested in the relation between intentionality and the self. The self is not a real [74] part of cogitation, as sensations are, for instance. The self is intimated in a cogitation in a very special manner which allows Husserl to consider its presence in consciousness as "a certain transcendence in the immanence of consciousness." "The pure ego is not an *Erlebnis* like the others, nor is it a constitutive part of an *Erlebnis*." [75]

The manner in which the ego relates to its acts must be the object of phenomenological descriptions.[76] But we should immediately point out that one should not misunderstand the phrase, "the ego relates to its acts," as if this relation were similar to that obtaining between objects or between consciousness and its objects; [77] this "transcendence within immanence" is a specific and irreducible structure.

We insist on the specificity of this "transcendence within immanence" to emphasize that the notion of the ego does not in any way prejudice the intentionality of consciousness. With the introduction of the ego, consciousness does not again become a "substance resting in itself" which would need intentionality in order to transcend itself: consciousness is first of all intentionality. It is only within the sphere of intentional consciousness, while respecting its transcendental mode of existing, that we can distinguish a subjective and an objective side, an ego and an object.[78] It is only as an internal character of intentionality that one can speak of an ego, of a point from which acts originate.

Let us summarize. The notion of the ego, which belongs to subjectivity in a manner quite different from the hyletic data, is in no way opposed to the notion of intentionality as the fundamental structure of consciousness; on the contrary, it presupposes it.

74. *Real* means here "constitutive of something's reality."
75. *Ideen*, § 57, p. 109.
76. *Ibid.*, § 80, p. 160.
77. *Ibid.*, p. 161.
78. *Ibid.*

4 / Theoretical Consciousness

WE HAVE SAID that intentionality is not the mere representation of an object. Husserl calls states of consciousness *Erlebnisse*—what is "lived" in the sense of what is experienced—and this very expression connects the notion of consciousness to that of life, i.e., it leads us to consider consciousness under the rich and multiform aspects characteristic of our concrete existence. The practical and aesthetic categories are, as we have asserted, part of the very constitution of being, in the same way as the purely theoretical categories.

However, it would be twisting Husserl's thought somewhat to speak here of equivalence. In Husserl's philosophy (and this may be where we will have to depart from it), knowledge and representation are not on the same level as other modes of life, and they are not secondary modes. Theory and representation play a dominant role in life, serving as a basis for the whole of conscious life; they are the forms of intentionality that give a foundation to all others.

The role played by representation in consciousness affects the meaning of intuition. This is what causes the intellectualistic character proper to Husserlian intuitionism. We cannot avoid here the study of the role of representation.

Husserl asserts the primacy of theoretical consciousness from the very beginning of his philosophy when he elaborates the concept of intentionality.[1] Although we have adopted here the point of view of *Ideen*, we must go back to the elaboration of

1. *LU,* II, fifth investigation.

[53]

the concept of representation in the *Logische Untersuchungen* and, taking into account Husserl's attitude in that work, compare the terminology of the *Logische Untersuchbungen* and that of *Ideen*.

We also need a brief survey of Husserl's attitudes in the *Logische Untersuchungen* and in *Ideen* respectively, in order to place these theses among the problems that were occupying him and to understand and evaluate them as a function of the views which they presuppose.

The attitude of the *Logische Untersuchungen* is a realist one. Although all consciousness is understood as consciousness of something, this "something" is conceivable outside of consciousness. Hence, the immanent analysis of consciousness finds only hyletic data (sensations—*Empfindungen*—as they are called in the *Logische Untersuchungen*), acts, and intentions,[2] while the correlates of those acts do not belong to consciousness but to the world of objects. The decisive step taken in *Ideen* is thinking through the idea of intentionality and seeing that the opposition between consciousness and objects makes no sense, and that it is in consciousness, in intentionality, that one finds the truly concrete and primary phenomenon which is the ground of the opposition between object and subject. Consequently, consciousness is described there in different terms, better to express its transcendental structure.

Ideen distinguishes, within consciousness, between, on the one hand, the hyletic data and the acts which animate them, and, on the other, those things of which consciousness is conscious. Husserl calls the subjective side of intentionality, the apprehensions (*Auffassungen*) which animate the hyletic data, *noeses*.[3] He opposes them to their correlate, those things of which consciousness is conscious, and calls these *noemata*.[4] However, the *noema* of consciousness is not identical with the object of consciousness. The relation between *noesis* and *noema* "cannot be that which is meant when one speaks of the relation between consciousness and its intentional objects." [5] The object of the perception of a tree is a tree, but the *noema* of this perception is its complete correlate, a tree with all the complexity of its predicates and especially of the modes in which it is given: a tree that is

2. *Ideen*, § 128, p. 266n.
3. *Ibid.*, § 85, p. 174.
4. *Ibid.*, § 88, p. 182.
5. *Ibid.*, § 129, p. 268.

green, lighted, given to perception or to an act of imagination, given clearly or indistinctly, etc. The *noema* of a tree is related to the tree as object. But the distinction the *Logische Unter-suchungen* makes between consciousness and its allegedly in-dependent object does not coincide with the distinction made here between objects and *noemata* of consciousness, because a *noema* is nothing else than an object considered through reflec-tion on the mode in which it is given. The correlative object can be recaptured on the basis of the elements which constitute a *noema.* Among them one distinguishes a core (*Kern*) of predi-cates which characterize the object which supports them; they form the *quid* of the object.[6] And these predicates are related to some sort of support, an X of which they are the predicates,[7] an "objective pole," a sort of "substance" which enters inevitably into the description of any object [8] and may remain identical while the predicates change. This X appears with its predicates once from one side, once from another.[9] The relation of consciousness to its object is the relation of a *noesis* as well as a *noema* [10] to an "object-pole." [11] In the perception of a tree, predicates such as green, tall, hard, and beautiful belong to the core.[12] But the core of the *noema* (which is called *matter* in the *Logische Unter-suchungen*) determines not only the object of consciousness, but also "what" consciousness grasps it "as"; that is, the marks or formal relations consciousness attributes to it. "It is the act's matter that makes its object count as this object and no other." [13] I may perceive the same Napoleon as "victor at Iena" or "van-quished at Waterloo." The object is identical, but the matter is different.

We must observe, among the characteristics of a *noema*, the mode in which the correlative object appears to consciousness: "die Weise wie es bewusst ist," [14] as, for example, the modes of "perceptively given" (*wahrnehmungsmässig*), "given in memory" (*erinnerungsmässig*), "given in a clear intuition" (*klaranschau-*

---

6. *Ibid.*, § 91, p. 189; § 129, p. 268.
7. *Ibid.*, § 131, pp. 270–71.
8. *Ibid.*, p. 272.
9. *Ibid.*, p. 271.
10. *Ibid.*, § 128, p. 266; § 129, pp. 267, 269.
11. *Ibid.*, § 129, pp. 268–69; § 131, p. 271.
12. *Ibid.*, § 129, p. 269.
13. *LU*, II, 416 [p. 589].
14. *Ideen*, § 130, p. 270; see also § 99, p. 209.

lich), etc. Let us note that this last type of character does not belong only to *noeses* but also to *noemata*. The words "memory," "perception," and "intuition" do not apply only to the subjective side of an intention but also characterize the objects themselves which, inasmuch as they are correlative to those acts, have the qualities of being remembered, perceived, or intuited.[15] It is with these qualities that objects form a *noema*.

The totality of the predicates that express the intended *quid*, with the marks and the categorial forms attributed to it, is called *matter* in the *Logische Untersuchungen* and the *sense* (*der Sinn*) of the *noema* in *Ideen*.[16] We must distinguish the notion of sense from that of *core*; the latter expresses a sense realized in intuition.[17]

The sense, considered in the totality of its modes of being conscious, forms what Husserl calls the "complete *noema*" (*das volle Noema*).[18] Since the distinction between *noema* and *noesis* has not yet been made explicitly in the *Logische Untersuchungen*, it is mainly the noetic correlate of the sense which Husserl has studied there under the term *matter*.[19]

Acts do not differ only by their matter or sense, since different acts may have the same sense. A perception, a memory, or an act of imagination may be directed toward the same object conceived in the same way,[20] toward the same "victor at Iena." What distinguishes those acts is the manner proper to each of them in which they posit their object, think of it as existing.[21] The fact of the act's positing its object is called in *Ideen* the *thesis* of the *noesis*.[22] The different acts which we have used as examples have different theses. The noematic correlate of a thesis is composed of those characters which form the complete *noema* and express the manner in which the object is given. In the *Logische Untersuchungen*, where the noematic aspect of acts has not yet been considered, the theses are studied under the "quality of acts." [23]

15. *Ibid.*, § 99, p. 209.
16. *Ibid.*, § 91, p. 189; § 93, p. 193; § 99, p. 208; § 129, p. 268; §133, p. 274.
17. *Ibid.*, § 132, p. 273.
18. *Ibid.*, § 90, p. 185; § 93, p. 193; § 94, p. 195; § 95, p. 198.
19. *Ibid.*, § 129, p. 268; § 94, p. 195.
20. *Ibid.*, § 91, p. 188.
21. *Ibid.*, § 94, p. 196; § 98, p. 208.
22. *Ibid.*, § 129, p. 268; § 133, p. 274.
23. *Ibid.*, § 129, p. 268.

Once we have defined these notions, we can easily show in what sense the theoretical relation to objects, the *theoretical thesis,* has, according to Husserl, a primacy in conscious life. We can then demonstrate how this primacy determines the nature of intuition.

Husserl starts from Brentano's assertion that all "acts are either representations or founded upon representations." [24] "Nothing can be desired, nothing can be hoped . . . if it is not represented." [25] While adopting this characteristic of Brentano's notion of intentionality, Husserl adds that the term *representation* is ambiguous and must first be analyzed to find an appropriate meaning for Brentano's assertion. Husserl's problem is to find which meaning of *representation* would allow him to accept Brentano's proposition.

For Brentano this proposition means that, in conscious life, either we have simple representations or, when we have other acts, such as judgments, hopes, desires, etc., their objects can be given only in a pure representation to which these acts must become bound to be directed toward their object. This relation between acts and representations is not a mere association but an intrinsic bond which forms a complex act directed toward a single object. Without representations these acts cannot exist. "An intentional experience [*Erlebnis*] gains objective reference only by incorporating an experienced act of presentation [*Vorstellen*] in itself through which *the object is presented* [*vorstellig macht*] *to it.*" [26]

Before going on, we must state at once that the fact that the objects of joy, will, etc., must be represented before being pleasant, wanted, etc., does not imply, for either Brentano or Husserl, a denial of the intentionality which is proper to these affective or volitional acts. In the *Logische Untersuchungen,* where the role of representation with respect to the constitution of objects is even more important than it is in *Ideen,* Husserl is opposed to any conception which would tend to say that

feeling, considered in itself, involves nothing intentional, that it does not point beyond itself to a felt object, that only its union

24. *LU,* II, 370 [p. 556]. This is representation as act, and not as object of representation. See F. Brentano, *Psychologie vom empirischen Standpunkt* (Hamburg: Felix Meiner, 1874), p. 111.

25. *LU,* II, 370 [p. 556]; Brentano, *Psychologie,* p. 109.

26. *LU,* II, 428 [p. 598].

with a presentation gives it a certain relation to an object, a relation only intentional by way of this connection and not intrinsically so.[27]

Husserl mentions Brentano's conception of the intentional character of feelings.

But we do not merely have a presentation, with an added feeling associatively tacked onto it and not intrinsically related to it, but pleasure or distaste direct themselves to the presented object and could not exist without such a direction.[28]

Let us return now to Brentano's notion of representation. According to Husserl, by representation Brentano means the act which Husserl later calls a "neutralized act," [29] whose nature consists in presenting a mere image of an object in which the object appears independently of any claim to exist or not exist.[30] Any Humean character of "belief" is missing. The image floats before us without our deciding about its existence or nonexistence.

According to Husserl, however, the analysis of intentionality shows that complex acts do not contain in themselves a representation in the sense defined above of "pure representation." A judgment is not the result of adding our agreement to a mere representation of this type and does not contain one in itself. A judgment has only the same sense or the same matter as a "mere representation." But matter does not exist independently of any quality, and a pure representation has itself a quality. It is the latter which, in a judgment, for instance, is replaced by the quality, the thesis of the judgment. We must therefore distinguish between the notion of "representation as matter" which different acts may have in common and the idea of representation as pure representation which is a quality, a thesis among other qualities and theses. It is representation as matter which must necessarily belong to any act and not the whole act of pure representation (quality and matter), as one could suppose from the first part of Brentano's proposition. "This second half by itself, i.e., every intentional experience is based on a presentation, has genuine self-evidence, if 'presentation' is interpreted as completed matter." [31]

27. *Ibid.*, p. 389 [p. 570].
28. *Ibid.*; see also *Ideen*, § 117, p. 241.
29. See a description of the phenomenon of neutralization in *Ideen*, §§ 109, 110, pp. 222 ff.
30. *Ibid.*, § 109, p. 223; § 111, p. 226.
31. *LU*, II, 458 [p. 621].

This theory, at the stage which we have just described, has not yet made the decisive step toward the assertion of the primacy of theoretical consciousness over all the other modes of reaching reality, over all the other types of intention. Indeed, that which in an act characterizes its particular mode of relating to an object, and correlatively the particular mode of existing of an object, is not the matter but the quality, the thesis, and the "complete *noema*," der Gegenstand in der Weise wie er gegeben ist." If Brentano's proposition is reduced to the assertion that any act is based on a representation understood as matter, as sense, then it does little more than assert the intentional character of acts of consciousness, without prejudging the mode in which reality is given. The theoretical mode of positing an object as existing is then of the same degree as any other, since it is also in need of a representation in the sense of "matter."

But Husserl goes further. Even if a "pure representation," as a complete act, cannot be found in perception or judgment, and if Brentano's proposition must be rejected when interpreted in this sense, Husserl thinks that he can still preserve Brentano's formulation in its entirety by considering another meaning of the term "representation."

Judgment and perception, as well as Brentano's "pure representation," are but species of Husserl's new concept of representation.

> But we can *employ the term* [representation] *to cover acts in which something becomes objective to us* [*in welchem uns etwas gegenständlich wird*] in a certain narrower sense of the word, one borrowed from the manner in which percepts and similar intuitions [32] grasp their objects in a single "snatch," or in a single "ray of meaning," or borrowed, likewise, from the one-term subject-acts in categorical statements, or from acts of straightforward hypothesis [*Akte des schlichten Voraussetzens*] serving as antecedents [*Vorderglieder*] in acts of hypothetical assertion, etc.[33]

Husserl calls these acts nominal, but he does not want to identify the mode of representation with the grammatical notion of name. The specific manner in which an object is thought in the act of naming it characterizes a wider sphere of acts, a sphere that goes beyond that of names.

32. Memory and imagination. See next chapter.
33. *LU*, II, 459 [p. 622].

In order to clarify this notion of representation, let us paraphrase some remarks of Husserl: That "S is P" is the correlate of the judgment which asserts it. But the same "fact that S is P," this *Sachverhalt*, as Husserl calls the correlate of a judgment, is given quite differently when, instead of judging (an act which is a synthesis of successive acts),[34] we take this *Sachverhalt* as subject or as the first term of a hypothetical judgment. "If S is P, Q is R." This second mode in which a *Sachverhalt* can be given is analogous to that of a subject in a judgment as well as to perception, and it is characterized by the unique ray which, in a hypothetical judgment, is directed toward the *Sachverhalt-as-first-term*.

By *name* Husserl does not mean substantives only. In analyzing the role of names of propositions, he finds that their primitive function is to be the subject of an assertion.[35] Therefore, if the act of representation is understood to be a nominal act, then according to Husserl, Brentano's proposition makes good sense. One may say "Each act is either itself a [re]presentation or founded on *one* or *more* [re]presentations."[36]

We have just distinguished the judgment concerning a *Sachverhalt* from the act which names it. Is it possible to maintain the unity of these acts despite this difference?

For Husserl, the difference is that the same *Sachverhalt* is once given as a synthesis being constituted in a "multiplicity of rays"[37] and once given in a single ray as an already-constituted synthesis. But this is a difference in matter (in sense) and not in quality (in the thesis). The difference between an act which names a *Sachverhalt* and an act that passes judgment on it is not in the mode of positing this *Sachverhalt* as existing but in its formal and categorial structure which, according to what we have said,[38] belongs to the matter. Moreover, the possibility of transforming the matter of a synthetic act, the "nominalization" of this act, as Husserl calls it,[39] is characteristic of any synthesis, for example, conjunctive, disjunctive, etc., and not only of the predicative synthesis of judgments. In all these acts, the many rays that are directed toward the various articulations of a syn-

34. *Ibid.*, pp. 472–73 [p. 632].
35. *Ibid.*, p. 463 [p. 625].
36. *Ibid.*, p. 461 [p. 625].
37. *Ideen*, § 119, p. 247.
38. See above.
39. *Ideen*, § 119, p. 248.

thesis can be transformed into a single ray [40] without affecting the quality of the act.

Judgments and nominal acts belong to the same type of acts, called objectifying acts (*objektivierende Akte*). It is within this group that one distinguishes between "names" and "judgments." With respect to the quality of objectifying acts, one distinguishes between thetic acts and acts with a neutralized thesis. We recognize under the latter term the "pure representations" which Brentano wanted to put at the basis of all conscious life, even of judgments. The representations are not distinct parts in an act of judgment but can be their neutralization. They have no primacy with respect to judgments, since they both form a species of the same genus of *objectifying acts*.

If we identify the concepts of "representation" and of "objectifying acts," we can, according to Husserl, preserve in its totality the value of Brentano's proposition. This proposition then means:

> *Each intentional experience is either an objectifying act* or has its basis in such an act, i.e., it must, in the latter case, contain an objectifying act among its constituents, whose total matter is individually the same as *its* total matter.[41]

This primacy of *objectifying acts,* or theoretical acts (since this notion is borrowed from the field of assertion), is explicitly asserted by Husserl.

> The reference to an object is, in general terms, constituted in an act's "matter." But all matter, according to our principle, *is the matter of an objectifying act and only through the latter can it* become the matter for a new act-quality founded upon this. We must after a fashion distinguish between secondary and primary intentions, the latter owing their intentionality to their foundation on the former.[42]

Husserl's conception of consciousness in the fifth investigation seems not only to imply the primacy of theoretical consciousness but also to see in it the sole access to what makes the being of objects. Of course—and we have already insisted on this—we should not forget those passages which assert the intentional character of nontheoretical acts. Acts of will, desire, affection,

40. *Ibid.*
41. *LU,* II, 493–94 [p. 648].
42. *Ibid.,* p. 494 [p. 648].

etc., indeed relate to objects. But, following the attitude of the *Logische Untersuchungen*, which considers only the noetic aspect of acts, it is difficult to see what those acts add to the constitution of objects. It seems that, according to the realist attitude of the *Logische Untersuchungen*, objectifying acts reach a being which exists independently of consciousness, and that the function of non-objectifying acts is to relate to these objects without contributing anything to their real constitution. It is only through matter that objects appear, but matter is always the matter of an objectifying act. Hence, the mode of existence of the existing world that is revealed to us is the same as that of objects given to our theoretical attention. *The real world is the world of knowledge.* The characters of "value," "usage," etc., attached to things are attributed to them by us but do not constitute their existence. At least, this is the attitude of the first edition of the *Logische Untersuchungen*. This is also why, in the third section of the sixth investigation, explicitly rejected in the second edition,[43] Husserl denies that propositions concerning desire, interrogation, or will express something that belongs to the sphere of objects. For him, these propositions are theoretical judgments of reflection, objectifying acts having conscious acts of interrogation, desire, etc., as their objects.

However, if we were able to speak differently in the preceding chapter, it is because Husserl later rejected these theses. The idea which has become central in the phenomenological attitude which is fully aware of itself, as we have it in *Ideen*, is that being is what is experienced, and that the reality it has in itself is always what it is for life in all the wealth of its modifications. This idea also compels us to put the structures correlative to non-objectifying acts among the characters of being and to speak of other modes of existence than that of theoretical objects. This idea allows us to go beyond the attitude of the *Logische Untersuchungen*.

We have spent some time discussing the attitude of the *Logische Untersuchungen* because the assertion of the dominant role of theory, perception, and judgment in our life, in which the world is constituted, is a thesis that Husserl has never abandoned. For him, representation will always be the foundation of all acts. Even if the objects of complex acts, such as will, desire, etc.,

---

43. See *LU*, III, foreword, p. vii [p. 664]; see also the new theory in *Ideen*, § 127, pp. 262 ff.

exist in another manner than do the objects of simple representation, they still must have to some extent the mode of existence of theoretical objects.[44] We must even add that in our opinion there is a difficulty here in Husserl's philosophy, the problem of understanding how to reconcile those two meanings of the existence of one and the same object.

For a theory of intuition, the primacy of theoretical consciousness is of the first importance, as we shall see later. The act of intuition, which brings us into contact with being, will be first and foremost a theoretical act, an objectifying act, and it remains so despite the modifications that *Ideen* will try to introduce in the notion of an objectifying act.

The notion of an objectifying act is borrowed from the sphere of assertions and therefore taints Husserl's intuitionism with intellectualism. However, placing judgment and perception under the same type of act,[45] and seeing judgment as only a new categorial formation which has the same quality as perception and naming, prepare the way for the intuitionist theory of truth, to which we shall devote the next chapter. For the first time, judgment and perception are brought together and put on the same level. This lets us surmise that truth must be identical in each of these acts and that the justification of a judgment has something in common with the justification of a perception.

44. *Ideen*, § 95, p. 198.
45. See *LU*, II, 15 [p. 259].

5 / Intuition

THE PRECEDING CHAPTER has shown that only an objectifying act has the privilege of giving us an object and that our contact with reality has the structure of a representation. But not all representations have the same right to posit their object as existing.[1] We may be dealing with purely imaginary objects or with objects that are "merely thought." Thought, for example, understood as a mental play that accompanies the comprehension of words, is also intentional; it is directed toward the object it means. But this does not say that this object exists, and thought cannot by itself posit the object's existence. The mode of consciousness or of representation through which we enter into contact with being has a determinate structure; it is, let us declare at once, intuition.

In order better to understand the structure of intuition, it may be useful to characterize "the merely signifying" mode of thought, which is the opposite mode of representation in which objects are meant without being given.

Husserl borrowed the concept of a "signifying act" from the realm of linguistic meaning. Any word or name has a meaning (*Bedeutung*), which is not a mere representation associated to the word but something to which the word or the name refers by means of a special intention.

> In virtue of such acts, the expression is more than a merely sounded word. It *means* something [*er meint etwas*] and, insofar

1. *Ideen*, § 135, pp. 280–81.

[65]

as it means something, it relates to what is objective [*auf Gegenständliches*].[2]

The intention of a word does not necessarily cause the object to be directly *seen* as it is in imagination or perception. For a word to have a meaning, it is enough that an object be meant.

We must remember this characteristic of signifying acts: their object is not seen or reached, it is only meant. As a matter of fact, signifying acts are the rule in ordinary discourse. Inasmuch as we have no image or perception, we content ourselves with the mere act of aiming at an object, at least provided that we understand what is said to us and what we ourselves say.

If we abstract from what Husserl calls the "level of the Logos"[3] (which is an added characteristic of the expressive acts which Husserl takes as a starting point), we end up with a more general notion of signifying acts which includes all acts aiming at, but not reaching, their object.

A signifying intention is empty or, so to speak, unrealized.[4] However, it can be realized in an image or a perception. Another type of act can indeed refer to the same object as is aimed at by a signifying intention. "It realizes [*erfüllt*], confirms, and illustrates more or less adequately the act of aiming, and therefore actualizes its relation to its object."[5]

But the difference between an intuitive act, which reaches its object, and a signifying act, which only aims at it, is not the difference between more or less clear or more or less explicit acts. Nonintuitive intentionality is more than an implicit allusion to an intuitive thought, a short cut to the fully realized act. We are not dealing with a difference in degree, as if we were op-

2. *LU*, II, 37 [p. 280].
3. To simplify matters, we abstract from what Husserl calls in *Ideen* "the level of the logos," which is some sort of character that any signifying intention must have in order to be expressed. A signifying act is not expressed unless it is internally modified for that purpose. In being expressed, it receives a sort of generality, a generality which individual objects themselves have when they are expressed and which must consequently be distinguished from the generality of abstract or ideal objects. See *Ideen*, § 124, p. 256; *LU*, III, 30 [p. 692].
4. *LU*, II, 38 [p. 281]; see also *Ideen*, § 136, pp. 282 ff.
5. *LU*, II, 38 [p. 281]. [This is only a paraphrase, not a literal quotation.—TRANS.]

posing a vague sketch or a pale image to a vivid and alive paint-ing.[6] To say that intuition actualizes the mere intention which aims at the object is to say that in intuition we relate directly to the object, we reach it. That is the entire difference between aim-ing at something and reaching it. A signifying intention does not possess its object in any way; it only thinks it. The following demonstrates that a signifying intention is not a confused intui-tion: when we think about a mathematical proposition, we may understand its meaning and analyze its various articulations— without, however, seeing with evidence the relations and the ideal objects which it expresses. "To make clear a thought to oneself . . . can . . . be achieved . . . by a signifying pres-entation." [7] Therefore, it is neither their confusion nor their ob-scurity that distinguishes signifying intentions from intuitions; it is rather, as we have already shown, their emptiness. They are characterized by their need for the fullness (*Fülle*) which is proper to intuition.[8] A signifying intention only thinks about an object, but intuition gives us something of the object itself. Even outside of perception (the privileged case of intuition), as in the case of imagination, intuition represents its object by analogy. A merely signifying intention alone "is 'in reality' no 'presenta-tion,' in it, nothing of the object comes to life." [9]

However, the *unsatisfied* character of empty intentions that we have mentioned may lead us to believe that an empty inten-tion is only the expectation of the apparition of an object. In-deed, expectations are intentions, but not all intentions are expectations. "It is not of its essence to be directed to future ap-pearances [*zukünftiges Eintreten*]." [10] When we look at the pat-tern of a rug that disappears under the furniture, we perceive only part of it directly, but the empty intentions directed from the perceived part toward the hidden part of the pattern do not in any way constitute an expectation.

The sphere of signifying acts includes the whole of conscious, representative life. We know different forms of it which corre-spond to all the forms of *objectifying acts*: perception, judgment, and conjunction (for example, A and B). We shall see that

6. *LU*, III, 76 [p. 728].
7. *Ibid.*, p. 68 [p. 722].
8. *Ibid.*, p. 76 [p. 728].
9. *Ibid.* [p. 729].
10. *Ibid.*, p. 40 [p. 700].

Husserl allows for the existence of an intellectual intuition able to grasp logical forms and categories. This is how far the sphere of signifying acts extends.

> To all acts of categorial intuition, with their categorially formed objects, purely significative acts may correspond. This is an obvious *a priori* possibility. There is no act-form relevant here to which there is not a corresponding possible form of meaning, and each meaning can be thought of as carried out without a correlated intuition.[11]

The sphere which we have just delineated is that of "thought," of "pure thought," as opposed to contact with things. Consciousness is intentionality, the relation to a transcendent being. But the concept of signifying intention allows us to understand why not all objects of thought are real, and it answers an objection which has certainly risen in the mind of the reader from the beginning of our discussion. Indeed, if we admit [12] that reality is that which is experienced, thought, believed, known, wanted, etc., are we not then led to giving the status of being to all the objects of our life, irrespective of the kind of act they are given in and irrespective of their meaning? Are we not giving up the distinction between true and false and thereby asserting the very impossibility of being mistaken?

The possibility of an act which relates to an object without reaching it, far from causing a confusion between existing objects of pure thought, helps us to understand the genuine meaning of the distinction. Pure thought is not directed toward some sort of purely immanent "mental image"; it is not opposed to direct contact with things, the contact which alone is a genuine transcendence. The difference between pure thought and contact with reality does not lie in their objects, and the problem of correlating them is fictitious. Intuition grasps the same object as is aimed at by a signifying act. *The difference does not lie in the object but in its mode of being given, of being experienced.* Pure thought is a modality of life at the same level as the presence to being. In signifying intentionality, consciousness transcends itself to the same extent as it does in its "presence to things." Contact with reality which guarantees the truth of sig-

11. *Ibid.*, p. 191 [p. 824].
12. According to chap. 2, above.

nifying acts is not a new intentionality which would have to transcend the allegedly immanent intentionality of the sphere of pure thought.

If knowledge is made up of acts of "pure thought" and of "contact with reality," it should be clear that knowledge is not something new, superimposed on the existence of subjects, but that it is one of their modalities, a determinate structure of intentionality. However, merely signifying acts are not, by themselves, knowledge. "In the purely symbolic understanding of a word, an act of meaning is performed (the word means something to us) but nothing is thereby known." [13] Knowledge will be the confirmation by an intuition of what was meant in the unfulfilled, merely signifying, intention. [14] There arises then the question of knowing the structure of intuitive acts.

Under the term intuitive acts, Husserl encompasses, on the one hand, perception (presentation, *Gegenwärtigung*) and, on the other, imagination and memory (re-presentation, *Vergegenwärtigung*). [15] These notions have in common that the objects meant by these acts are *themselves* given and not only meant. They are acts "in which objects . . . are given in person [*zur Selbstgegebenheit kommen*]." [16] *One should therefore not include in the concept of intuition the notion of "sensible" or that of "immediate," in the sense of "given prior to any positive action of the mind"; one should not oppose intuition to "intellection," but one should insist on the fact that intuition is an act which possesses its object.* This is what is expressed by the concept of *Fülle*, fullness, which characterizes intuitive acts, as opposed to the "emptiness" of signifying acts. [17]

The notion of fullness expresses the fact that the determinations of objects are present to consciousness. But in the immanent constitution of intuitive acts Husserl attributes the function of representing the fullness of objects to some special contents, and these contents he also calls "fullness" (*Fülle*). [18]

The notion of *Fülle* as a real constituent of acts is identified in the *Logische Untersuchungen* with sensations (*Empfindun-*

13. *LU,* III, 33 [p. 694].
14. *Ibid.,* p. 34 [p. 695].
15. On the relation between imagination and memory, see *Ideen,* §§ 111, 112, pp. 225 ff.
16. *Ibid.,* § 1, p. 7; § 67, p. 126; § 136, p. 283.
17. *Ibid.,* § 136, p. 283.
18. *LU,* III, 76 [p. 728].

gen). We have already emphasized all that differentiates them from the "sensations" of sensualism, and we have especially insisted that sensations must not be confused with the qualities of external objects, since they each belong to a different level of reality, one being represented, the other being experienced. Nevertheless, for Husserl, sensations are elements which, in life, represent objects, although only with the help of intentionality.[19] Sensations are characterized as "reflections and shadows" (*Abschattungen*) of objects.[20] They are called "sensations" in the case of perception (presentation), and "phantasms" in the case of memory and imagination (re-presentation). These elements constitute the fullness of acts and are analogues of the objects they represent in imagination or present in perception.[21] The totality of sensations and phantasms included in any act (an intuitive act is not always a pure perception or pure re-presentation but is constituted by a set of perceptual, imaginative, and other elements) delineates the concept of "the intuitive content of an act" (*intuitiver Gehalt des Aktes*).[22]

Having determined the concept of *Fülle*, we can understand why there are gradations of intuitive acts and in which direction these gradations go. First, an intuitive act may have before it a more or less large number of characters of the object toward which it is directed. It merely aims at the others. While we think about a person, a more or less large number of his features may reappear before us and the rest of his face be only thought. Furthermore, "intuitive contents" may be more or less vivid and thus more or less analogous to the object. Finally, these intuitive elements may include more or fewer perceptual contents or sensations which give the object-itself and do not simply reflect it, as phantasms do. Hence we distinguish, in an act, degrees of extension, vividness, and reality.[23] These are three directions in which the intuitive content may tend toward an ideal, and this ideal is the act of perception. In perception the fullness realizes for us an object as it is in-itself. Perception is characterized by the fact that it has its object "in flesh and bones" (*leibhaft-gegeben*) before it. Thus it is a privileged intuitive act, a primary

19. *Ideen*, § 36, p. 65; § 41, p. 75.
20. *Ibid.*, § 41, p. 75.
21. *LU*, III, 79 [p. 731].
22. *Ibid.*
23. *Ibid.*, p. 83 [p. 734]; see also *Ideen*, § 68, pp. 127–28.

intuition, as Husserl calls it.[24] Perception gives us being. It is through reflecting on the act of perception that we must seek the origin of the very notion of being.[25]

The analysis of intuitive acts, as we have performed it so far, has shown that their characteristic property is to give objects. The *Fülle* has appeared as the element of these acts that fulfills this function.[26] Now, since the notion of *Fülle* is tied to that of sensation, a purely immanent element of consciousness, are we not falling back into Berkeleian idealism? If the existence of an object given in an intuitive act means only the presence in the mind of some immanent, intuitive contents, then the latter do constitute the genuine, real objects. In that case, consciousness would no longer be this eminently concrete phenomenon which has a *sui generis* mode of existence and in which objects are found as objects intended or meant (*gemeint*) by consciousness. Consciousness would become once again a sphere of contents representative of objects, whose intentional transcendence would be only an illusion. In other words, objects would exist not by virtue of an intention which gives them meaning as being, but by virtue of the presence, in a flow of inanimate states, of certain contents called *sensations*. Under such conditions, intuition would no longer be characterized as being a special mode of intentionality but as essentially a special type of immanent content.

One must admit, at least in our opinion, that in the role which Husserl attributes to "intuitive contents," and especially in his conception of them as *analogous* to transcendent objects as their reflection,[27] there are echoes of British empiricism,[28] as we have mentioned already. But we have also shown that consciousness in Husserl is not the same as subjectivity in British empiricism. Most important, Husserl's theory of intuitive acts, the first half of which we have summarized, is radically opposed to any attempt to characterize intuition by the hyletic elements of consciousness.

24. *Ideen*, § 1, pp. 7–8; § 39, p. 70; § 43, p. 79; § 67, p. 126; § 136, p. 282; and *passim*.

25. *Ibid.*, § 47, p. 89.

26. On the role of sensation in perception, see also *ibid.*, § 97, p. 203.

27. *Ibid.*, p. 202; and *passim; LU*, III, 92–93 [pp. 741–42].

28. *Ideen*, § 86, p. 176.

Indeed, we have shown [29] that all acts are made up of "matter" and "quality" ("sense" and "thesis," understood as the structure of the *noema* and the *noesis,* using the terminology of *Ideen*). But the fullness is not something unrelated to these elements of conscious activity.

> Matter and fulness are, however, by no means unrelated and, when we range an intuitive act alongside a signitive act to which it brings fulness, the former act does not differ from the latter merely by the joining on of a third distinct moment of fulness to the quality and matter common to the two acts.[30]

First, signifying acts themselves are not simply made up of matter and quality. "An act of signification is only possible insofar as intuition becomes endued with a new intentional essence [31] whereby its intuitive object points beyond itself [*über sich hinausweist*] in the manner of a sign." [32] For example, the perception of a linguistic sound in a conversation gives an intuitive basis to the meaning of the words. Hence an intuition is necessary before a meaning can occur. But, as Husserl explains immediately, it is only a sensible "intuitive content" which is needed and not a complete act. The same "intuitive content" which serves as the basis for a meaning could also serve as *Fülle* for an intuitive act. The intuitive content, the "representative" as Husserl calls it,[33] may therefore have a signifying as well as an intuitive function. Where does the difference lie which separates them?

According to Husserl, the specific function of a representative depends on the form of its relation to the matter of an intentional act. Husserl calls this form the "form of representation," and he calls the unity of matter and the "representative" "representation." [34] The form of representation expresses the manner in which intentionality takes possession of a representative. This is why Husserl also calls it "apprehension."

29. See above, chap. 4.
30. *LU*, III, 88 [p. 738].
31. Intentional essence, in the terminology of *LU*, means quality plus matter.
32. *LU*, III, 89 [p. 739].
33. *Ibid.*, p. 90 [p. 739].
34. We put the word "representation" in quotation marks in order to distinguish it from the word *representation* in chap. 4, where it was the translation of the German *Vorstellung*.

From this, we can see that the essential characteristic of intuition is also a characteristic of intentionality. *The signifying or intuitive role of a representative depends on the intention which animates it, on the irreducible sense given to it by intentionality.*[35] This difference in the manner of animating a representative is not reducible to anything else. "The difference between signifying and intuitive apprehension is an irreducible phenomenological difference." [36] Although the internal structure of a signifying act is characterized by the indifference of the representative with respect to the object meant by the matter, and although there is in intuitive acts a relation of analogy between the two, in the last analysis the two acts are distinguished by the mode of the relation between the representative and the matter. According to Husserl, representatives, even when analogous to their objects, may function as signifying contents.[37]

Hence, if perception reaches being itself, being "in person," if it is in perception that we are in direct relation to reality, it is due to the specific character and meaning of perceptual intentionality.[38]

> The intentional character of perception, as opposed to the mere representation of imagination, is that of direct presentation. This is, as we know, an internal difference of acts, more precisely, of their interpretative form.[39]

After making these preliminary considerations, we shall now try to determine the role played by intuition in the realm of truth.

Meanings aim at their objects; intuition, and in particular perception, reaches them. The objects of both may be identical, as may be their matter or sense, since meanings aim at the same objects as the corresponding intuitions; the way "in which" these objects are aimed at or perceived may also be identical.[40] The two acts may, therefore, overlap, so to speak, and an object which was meant only in an empty meaning may become seen in in-

---

35. On the role of intentionality in the *hyle,* see *Ideen,* § 98, p. 206.
36. *LU,* III, 93 [p. 742]. [This is a paraphrase, not an exact quotation.—TRANS.]
37. *Ibid.,* p. 54 [p. 711].
38. *Ideen,* § 43, pp. 79–80.
39. *LU,* III, 116 [p. 761].
40. See *Ideen,* § 136, p. 283; § 140, p. 291.

tuition; a signifying and empty intention may become in some way fulfilled. Husserl speaks here of the phenomenon of *Erfüllung*, which we translate by the term *realization*. As fullness is more or less perfect, so is realization. In adequate perception we have a perfect realization of a significant intention. A meaning, a mere thought, which could make no pronouncement concerning an object—not about its nature or about its existence—now faces, in realization, this object itself, and sees it exactly the way in which it was aiming at it. *"The object is actually 'present' or 'given,' and present as just what we have intended it; no partial intention remains explicit and still lacking fulfillment."* [41] What happens here is therefore a genuine *adaequatio rei et intellectus*. For example, I think about a roof covered with red tiles, without seeing it, without even imagining it; I look up and see this roof exactly as I was thinking it. This is a realization of my original thought. The roof, as I was thinking it, is directly in front of my eyes—is present *in person*.

In this example, the realization confirms the original intention. However, instead of being confirmed, the original intention could also be invalidated. Perception may "disappoint" (*enttäuschen*) a signifying intention. For instance, I may intend "the red roof of this house in front of me," yet when I look up, the roof may happen to be green. There is dissonance (*Widerstreit*) between the object of meaning and that of intuition, and we end with the negation of what was assumed by mere meaning: the roof is not red. This dissonance between the object-meant and the object-given must still be based on a common element. To have opposition there must be partial agreement. "Disappointment" (Enttäuschung) is possible only where there is a partial realization. *"An intention can only be frustrated in conflict insofar as it forms part of a wider intention whose completing part is fulfilled."* [42]

This is why dissonance may be understood as a type of *realization*. An object must be given for a dissonance to arise, and even if a signifying meaning is disappointed there is room for truth. Dissonance is not simply the absence of intuitive fullness, a merely privative notion. But dissonance is, on the basis of a partial agreement, a positive phenomenon, a synthesis which ends in knowledge, although this synthesis is negative.

41. *LU*, III, 118 [p. 762].
42. *Ibid.*, p. 43 [p. 702].

Consciousness of the realization or the disappointment of a signifying intention is evidence. Evidence, therefore, is not a purely subjective feeling accompanying certain psychic phenomena.[43] Evidence is a form of intentionality in which an object is facing consciousness *in person* and in the same guise as it was meant. If we say that evidence is the criterion of truth, we do not mean that evidence is only a subjective index of truth; we do not mean that being could appear in such a way as to invalidate the most certain evidences. Evidence is defined precisely by the fact that it is the presence of consciousness in front of being. There is the very origin of the notion of being.

> If someone experiences the self-evidence of A, it is self-evident that no second person can experience the absurdity of the same A, for that A is self-evident, means that A is not merely meant, but also genuinely given, and given as precisely what it is thought to be. In the strict sense, it is itself present. But how could a second person refer in thought to this same thing A, while the thought that it is A is genuinely excluded by a genuinely given non-A?[44]

If intuition is the central element of knowledge, do we not face an insuperable difficulty once we must speak about the truth of judgments? Indeed, the intentional correlate of the judgment, "the tree is green," is not an object "tree" that a judgment must relate to another object "greenness." [45] It is a *Sachverhalt* which is intended by this complex act: the "fact that the tree is green" (*das Grünsein des Baumes*). This *Sachverhalt* is an object made up of other objects that constitute it, such as "tree" and "greenness," objects which in turn are related to each other in a certain way. This relation also belongs to an objective sphere of intention and is not a purely subjective relation between representations. A relation between representations is not yet a representation of a relation.

These *Sachverhalte* are constantly objects of our concrete life; to live is not just to perceive but also to judge. Especially in scientific life, we constantly encounter *Sachverhalte*. A *Sachverhalt*, as the object of sensible perception, belongs to the domain of being if it is true that we find the origin of all notions of being in the objects of concrete life. To be has a different meaning here

43. *Ideen,* § 21, pp. 39–40; § 145, p. 300; *LU,* I, 180 ff. [pp. 187 f.].
44. *LU,* III, 127 [p. 769].
45. *Ideen,* § 94, p. 194.

from the one it had in the domain of objects of sensible perception, and we shall soon make this meaning more precise.

The structure of a *Sachverhalt* shows us that among the constituents of being there are not only sensible objects but also categories, such as the predicative category expressed in judgments by the word "is." Furthermore, prior to a judicative synthesis, even simple objects, objects expressed by a name, for example, are not themselves without a certain categorial form.

> In our meanings, therefore, parts of very different kinds are to be found, and among those we may here pay special attention to those expressed by formal words such as "the," "a," "some," "many," "few," "two," "is," "not," "which," "and," "or," etc., and further expressed by the substantival and adjectival, singular and plural inflection of our words.[46]

Let us first remark that there is an essential difference between these forms and the matter which they encompass. Let us try to delineate these forms. The propositions which express the world of our perception may be reduced to their formal skeletons. We thus obtain expressions like "S is P," "S and P," "S or P," "an S," "two Ps," etc. Only the letters S and P above express sensible contents of perception. Even if we admit that the "terms" which the letters replace are complex and allow separation into form and matter,[47] we must suppose in the last analysis that there are simple terms. These terms constitute the matter which is directly realized in perception. Although forms may be a constitutive part of a matter, as when a *Sachverhalt* serves as subject for a new judgment ("I assert that the tree is green"), we have said that forms have an essentially different function than matter and delineate the categorial sphere. Only matter can be directly given in a perceived object. Terms, however, such as "is," "and," "or," "one," etc., cannot be found in objects in the same way.

Indeed, "being-as-copula," for example, is not a real predicate of objects. "Being is nothing *in* the object, no part of it, no moment tenanting it, no quality or intensity of it, no figure of it or internal form whatsoever, no constitutive feature of it." [48] The

46. *LU*, III, 129 [p. 774].
47. Matter does not here have the meaning it had in chap. 4. Here it is opposed to categorial form. In this case, Husserl calls it *Stoff*.
48. *LU*, III, 137 [p. 780].

copula is not a character of objects that is either one of their constitutive parts, such as sound or color, or is superimposed on them, such as a melody on the set of sounds which constitute it. A certain melody is tied to certain sounds as its matter. But the essential characteristic of a categorial form like "being-as-copula" is precisely to be indifferent to the matter which it encompasses. The conjunctive form "and" and the disjunctive form "or," or the form "something," can be indifferently applied to all types: we may think about "a man and an animal," "a perception and a memory," "Neptune and mathematical adequacy."

It is because categorial forms are not part of the content of objects (as are color and intensity) that we have been led to seek their roots in acts of consciousness and to attribute to reflection only the awareness of their discovery. This is, for example, the interpretation which has often been given to Kant's synthesis: [49] in the multiplicity of disparate data, understood as contents of consciousness, the spontaneity of the mind functions by relating these data to each other, while an act of reflection allows us to grasp this very act of relating. In this sense, the synthesis does not belong to the sphere of objectivity but is solely an internal character of acts of consciousness. Husserl is opposed to such a conception of categorial forms.[50] According to him, they belong to the sphere of objects. "As the concept *Sensuous Object* . . . cannot arise through reflection upon perception . . . , so the concept of State of Affairs cannot arise out of reflection on judgements." [51] "Not in these *acts as objects*, but in *the objects of these acts*, do we have the abstractive basis which enables us to realize the concepts in question." [52] We have already intimated this.

A categorial form is not a real predicate of things or the result of a reflection on consciousness. It is an ideal structure of objects. Categorial forms must, however, be distinguished from the *ideal essences* of individual objects. The genus of an object is not its form.[53] The essence "color" is not the form of red or blue but their genus. Their form would be "something in general." A form is not the object of a higher level of generalization with respect

49. See Husserl, *Philosophie der Arithmetik* (Halle: Pfeffer, 1891), pp. 36 ff.

50. *LU*, III, 160–61 [p. 799].

51. *Ibid.*, pp. 140–41 [p. 783].

52. *Ibid.*, p. 141 [pp. 783–84].

53. *Ideen*, § 13, p. 26.

to which all higher genera would only be species: [54] it transcends generality.[55] "Categories cannot be found in material singularizations in the same manner as red in general can be found in the various nuances of red, or as 'color' in red and blue." [56]

Truths which depend only on the form of objects Husserl calls *analytic*,[57] in contrast to material synthetic truths, which are founded on a higher genus. We shall return to this.[58]

In one of the most decisive passages of his philosophy, Husserl presents the notion of categorial form, together with the distinction between substrative forms and the syntactical forms (relation, conjunction, predication, etc.) which presuppose them,[59] and the clearly affirmed opposition between the formal and the general. Without stopping here for a detailed analysis of forms, let us say only that forms are the subject matter of logic. Since forms have been distinguished from genera, logic is decisively separated from ontology. Logic which deals with the general form of being can say nothing of its material structure;[60] logic therefore lies outside of any psychology (since forms are forms of objects) and is also independent of any science which studies those objects, since logic is concerned only with their form. However, it is not Husserl's logic which interests us here. It is enough, for a theory of intuition, to delineate the notion of categorial form as we have just done.

When we return to the theory of intuition, it is clear that to reconcile the theory of truth (which sees truth in intuition) with the fact that a *Sachverhalt* is also constituted by means of categories, we shall have to speak of categorial or intellectual intuition. This leads us to one of the most interesting points in Husserl's theory.

Let us remember that we have asserted from the beginning that the concept of intuition is defined, not by means of characters that are proper to sensible perception, but by the fact that intuition realizes a meaning; it is defined as evidence. Is it possible to distinguish, from the way in which categorial forms are

54. *Ibid.*
55. See above, chap. 1, p. 4.
56. *Ideen*, § 13, p. 27.
57. *Ibid.*, § 10, p. 22.
58. See below, p. 116.
59. *Ideen*, § 11, p. 24.
60. *Ibid.*, § 10, pp. 21–22.

given, between what is "merely meant" and what is "intuitively given?"

Husserl answers affirmatively. "There must at least be an act which renders identical services to the categorial elements of meaning that merely sensuous perception renders to the material elements." [61] There is an act directed in a favored manner at categorially formed objects, an act which has a *direct view* of them and of their particular form. We can therefore enlarge the notion of intuition, because its function, in the sphere of categories, is analogous to that which it performs in the sensible sphere. There is a profound similarity between sensible intuition and categorial intuition. In both acts, consciousness faces being directly; "Something appears as 'actual,' as 'self-given.' " [62]

Sensibility and understanding, inasmuch as they reveal truth, can be subsumed under the single concept of an intuitive act. Nevertheless, we still must account for their difference and show especially that this difference is extrinsic to the intuitive or non-intuitive character of these acts.

We find in Husserl an attempt at delineating what is called sensibility and understanding, an attempt which is interesting because of the method used. Husserl does not try to characterize them by means of purely extrinsic marks, such as innateness or the use of the sense organs. In order to distinguish sensibility from understanding. Husserl begins, not with some naïve metaphysics or anthropology, but from the intrinsic meaning of sensible or categorial life itself.

Sensible objects are given directly; they are constituted "in schlichter Weise." [63] The acts which give them to us do not require other acts on which they are to be founded. They are, so to speak, of a single degree. "In sense-perception the 'external' thing appears 'in one blow,' as soon as our glance falls upon it." [64] We have more than once commented on the complex character of the perception of external things, on the infinite continuum of acts which is required in order to grasp them. But each element in this sequence, each "one-sided view," is given "all at once" and represents *the whole of its object*. It is the same book which I know more or less well. I have immediately a complete act of

61. *LU*, III, 142 [p. 785].
62. *Ibid.*, p. 143 [p. 785].
63. *Ibid.*, p. 145 [p. 787].
64. *Ibid.*, p. 147 [p. 788].

knowledge of this book. Furthermore, the unity of the successive looks which are taken at the same object is not a new act, a synthesis based on these simple acts. The unity does not constitute an object of higher degree. The sensible perception of things is necessarily "schlicht," no matter what the degree of perfection of their continuous and successive apprehension. The successive acts fuse and do not remain separate as if waiting for a new act to perform their synthesis. The unity of these acts is a whole in which the constitutive articulations have disappeared. The multiplicity of acts of perception is like a single stretched-out act, and in this stretched-out act "nothing new is objectively meant . . . but the same object is continuously meant in it, the very object that the part-percepts *taken singly* were already meaning." [65] If the object of these successive acts is constantly reidentified, it is not this reidentification which is the object of the sum of the acts. An act may of course be directed toward this identity itself, but this act would have a new structure and would no longer have any of the characteristics of sensible intuition.

What characterizes categorial as opposed to sensible perception is that the former is necessarily founded on sensible perceptions. Acts such as that of "conjunction" or "disjunction" constitute new forms of objects which, in essence, could not be given in "schlichte" acts which grasp their objects all at once. *They have an essential relation to the sensible contents on which they are based.* "Their manner of appearance is essentially determined by this relation. We are here dealing with a sphere of objects [*Gegenständlichkeit*] *which can only show themselves 'in person' in such founded acts.*" [66] The character of being "founded," together with their *sui generis* relation to the act and to the correlative objects on which they are founded, characterize the mode of appearing and existing of ideal objects. This mode, however, is different in the case of categories and in that of ideal essences. In the intuition of categorial forms, the object founded includes in itself the objects which found it. A *Sachverhalt* contains, in some way, the things that constitute it; essences, on the contrary, although they are founded on sensible perception, do transcend it in some way. We shall devote a chapter to the intuition of essences. For the time being, let us come back to categorial intuition, which we may understand better through

---

65. *Ibid.*, p. 150 [p. 790]; see also *Ideen*, § 11, p. 24.
66. *LU*, III, 146 [p. 788].

an example. Let us consider a sensible perception A and another sensible perception directed toward *a* which is part of A. As long as we stay at the level of sensible perception, we cannot conceive *a* "*qua* part" of A. This would require a new intention of thought that would precisely let *a* appear *qua* part of A. This act, directed toward the partitive character of *a*, presupposes the perception of *a* and of A and gives their unity a new sense. It is a categorial act having precisely for its object the part-whole relation. The part is in the whole and is given in the perception of the whole but not *qua* part, a character which can be constituted only by a founded act.[67]

These considerations are of great interest because they clarify the problem of intuition. But before examining them from that angle, we must also see that they are not without importance from certain other points of view.

They clarify many aspects of the problem of the relation between sensibility and understanding. Indeed, one seems to find there a deep antinomy: the spontaneity of the mind which characterizes categorial acts appears to perform a creation that goes beyond sensible perception, yet the objects of logical thought seem to belong to the objective sphere. One is then naturally led to ask how it happens that the product of our mind's spontaneity agrees with real objects, with those categories which seem, so to speak, to be in sensible objects.[68]

This antinomy presupposes a certain concept of objectivity, a concept too rigid to express the content of life. The concept's rigidity consists in always conceiving the objectivity of being according to one type and at one level. It consists in not admitting degrees or, rather, different modes of objectivity. This concept of objectivity forces us to seek categorial forms in the midst of sensible beings or to consider forms as attributes of being in the same sense in which we attribute sound and color to being. Husserl goes beyond this notion of an object. An object must be understood in the widest, most formal sense of the term, that which only expresses its function of being the subject of a true assertion.[69] To denote this concept, Husserl chooses the vaguer term "objectivity" (*Gegenständlichkeit*), by which he under-

67. *Ibid.*, p. 155 [p. 794].
68. Concerning what we have said above about the fact that categories belong to the objective sphere, see p. 77.
69. *Ideen*, § 22, p. 40; *LU*, II, 101 [p. 330].

stands not only "objects in the narrower sense, but . . . also
. . . states of affairs [*Sachverhalt*], properties [*Merkmal*], and
non-independent forms,[70] etc., whether real or categorial." [71] Defined thus by its most general function, objectivity can perfectly
admit of the idea of different levels of being, different meanings
of the term "to exist." [72]

By returning to the intuitive intentionality which presents to
us these different forms of being, we have in our analysis of
sensibility and understanding tried to show what is meant by the
being of categorial forms and by the new "objectivity" formed by
them. Given in founded acts, they do not add a new sensible
property to an object but they determine it in a *new dimension of
being.*

> They can do nothing to them, cannot change them in their own
> being, since the result would otherwise be a new object in the pri-
> mary real [73] sense [*im primären und realen Sinne*]. Evidently the
> outcome of a categorial act, e.g., one of collection or relation, con-
> sists in an objective "view" [*Fassung*] of what is primarily intuited,
> a "view" that can only be given in such a founded act, so that the
> thought of a straightforward [*schlicht*] percept of the founded ob-
> ject, or of its presentation through some other straightforward in-
> tuition is a piece of nonsense.[74]

The problem of the concordance between sensible reality and
logical thought [75] is absurd, because sensible reality is not sup-
posed to correspond to logical thought but to serve as a basis for
it. A "categorial objectivity" has a relation to sensible objects as
its basis and is inconceivable without them, because such a relation to sensible objects is inherent to its very mode of existing,
although it exists in a totally new way. Furthermore, although
sensible objects include by nature the possibility of those categorial objects which are based on them, they are not themselves affected by these categorial forms the way they would be if
we were to modify the pattern of their existence (the way a

70. Concerning this term, see below, p. 109.

71. *LU*, II, 38n [p. 281].

72. *Ideen*, § 22, p. 40.

73. *Real* here refers to the existence of a *res*, a thing, i.e., a sensible object.

74. *LU*, III, 186 [p. 820].

75. See Hermann Lotze, *Logik: Drei Bücher vom Denken, vom
Untersuchen und vom Erkennen* (Leipzig: S. Hirzel, 1874), pp.
536 ff.

potter gives form to clay).[76] Categorial functions, "in 'forming' sensible objects, leave their real essence untouched." [77]

This theory of intuition places truth and reason in the primary presence of objects to consciousness. But the idea of an object is used here in a sense which is wide enough to admit different levels of being. Being is not thereby reduced to the world of sensible perception, and its originality is respected. The meaning of the existence of *Sachverhalte* lies in the specific manner in which they are given to consciousness and becomes explicit once this manner is analyzed.

However, the interest of these phenomenological analyses does not consist primarily in clarifying the relationship between sensibility and understanding or in providing us with an example of how phenomenology poses and resolves such a problem; the interest of these analyses consists mainly in showing that the distinction between sensibility and understanding can be made by means of characteristics that are not related to intuition. Thus, intuition cannot be the privilege of sensibility. The specific function of sensibility in conscious life cannot therefore be identified with the function of intuition. Our analyses have tried to show the role played by such synthetic acts as judgments in giving us access to being, i.e., knowledge. We see more clearly what we have already asserted, i.e., that the specific judicative function is not the essential component of knowledge, that it is not with judgment that truth begins. The function of judgments is quite different. It consists in constituting a new form of objects, a new level of being. The only way we can speak of truth and falsity with respect to judgments is according to whether or not they can be realized in intuition.

Intuition, however, understood as direct vision of objects, seems to be independent of whether it takes place in a sensible or in an intellectual act. Is it then a truly essential phenomenon which can be made into a new concept? Is it not a purely formal and verbal extension of the notion of sensible intuition, since inside the intuitive sphere the intuition of a *Sachverhalt* is different from that of a sensible object, and thereby introduces in it an element of "discursion"? Husserl explicitly protests against such an objection.[78] In this theory, he is not interested in deciding

76. *LU*, III, 186 [p. 820].
77. *Ibid.*, p. 185 [p. 819].
78. *Ibid.*, p. 165 [p. 803]; *Ideen*, § 3, p. 11.

between the mediated or immediate character of knowledge or in determining the respective places of intuition and discursion in knowledge. He is not interested in assimilating them to each other, as, for example, in assimilating the intuitive knowledge of inventors (some sort of intellectual feeling) to demonstrative knowledge [79] or vice versa. Husserl is preoccupied by a quite different problem. *The problem is to go back to the original phenomenon of truth in order to understand its very essence,* to return to the phenomenon which alone makes possible these distinctions between mediated and immediate knowledge. Husserl is not interested in assimilating intelligence and sensibility to each other; hence he insists strongly on their difference while trying to account for it. He wants only to shed light on the aspect by which these activities of the mind are susceptible of truth. This aspect is intuition, understood as an intentionality whose intrinsic meaning consists in reaching its object and facing it as existing.

In order to emphasize the deep philosophical interest of this last point, we shall introduce some historical remarks, without pretending to cover the history of the subject or to exhaust the wealth of tradition. We shall only draw a few schematic lines which, because of their very sketchiness, will be that much more able to help us delineate Husserl's attitude.

We have inherited, from the ancient tradition since Parmenides, the idea that truth lies in the adequacy of thought to things. Moreover, since Aristotle,[80] truth and falsity are considered the exclusive privilege of judgments, which are the assertion of a relation between a subject and a predicate. For the knowledge of first principles (knowledge which was not a judgment), Aristotle allowed another type of truth; but this was a type of knowledge which did not admit of being false.[81]

We believe that this idea of "adequation" is the source of all difficulties and of all problems. What does "adequation" between mind and things mean? Is not adequation possible only where there is a common measure? Even if we admit that it makes

79. See Albert Spaier, *La Pensée concrète* (Paris: Alcan, 1927), pp. 261 ff.; and also E. Goblot, "Expérience et intuition," *Journal de psychologie,* XXII (1928), 721–34.

80. *De Interpretatione* I. 16a12. *De Anima* III 8. 432a11. These references are taken from Eduard Zeller, *Philosophie der Griechen,* 4th ed. (Leipzig: Reisland, 1921), II, pt. 2, 191.

81. See Zeller, *Philosophie der Griechen,* pp. 191, 219.

sense to speak of a resemblance between thought and things, how can we, from the point of view of a subject who knows truth, make sure of this correspondence, since in *knowledge* objects are always given by the *intellectus*? It seems that one must conclude that the adequation of thought to things must be discovered in some determinate structures of thought. The logos must be constituted according to a law. It is logic which will formulate the laws of reasonable thought, i.e., the laws of a thought which is adequate to its object. The laws of logic which allow us to bind subject and predicate become the very law of reality. This conception is then based on a metaphysical thesis which says that the principles of judgment are at the same time the principles of being. This thesis will become a problem for Kant.

This road leads to rationalism. From this follows the absolutely unintelligible character of judgments of fact and the almost hybrid secondary character of the truth of fact. Leibniz states:

> Res se habet velut in legibus serierum aut naturis linearum, ubi in ipso initio sufficiente progressu omnes continentur. *Talemque opportet esse totam naturam alioque inepta foret et indigna sapiente.*[82]

We believe that it is not the contingency of truths of fact against which rationalism rebels; it is not the need for necessary truths which obliges rationalism to suspect empiricism; for rationalism, the very notion of truth seems to be identical with that of intelligibility understood as a logical tie between concepts.[83]

The rationalism of Leibniz seems, on this point, more coherent with itself and it fully realizes the identification of truth and a priori truth, understanding the latter as that which obeys only the law of contradiction. Perfect science, i.e., perfectly rational science, is a priori science. The "a priori" is interpreted as the independence from all experience, as the justification by virtue of the sole intrinsic force of understanding. In his *Erkenntnisproblem,* Cassirer says that, for Leibniz,

> a concept may be possible and true without its content's being ever given in external reality inasmuch as we have the certainty that

82. Leibniz, *Oeuvres*, ed. C. I. Gerhardt, 7 vols. (Berlin: Weidman, 1875–90), II, 258. "Letter to De Bolder," November 10, 1703. My italics.

83. See Octave Hamelin, *Essai* (Paris: Alcan, 1907), pp. 6–7.

it can be used as a starting point and a source for valid judgments because it has no internal contradiction.[84]

The foundation of truth always lies in an internal tie between ideas, the tie between subject and predicate. Even the intuitions which must be at the origin of these deductions are considered intuitions only by naïve science. This is where logic is inserted, in order to go further and demonstrate these principles themselves: [85]

> Nothing is without reason; all truths have an a priori proof derived from the notion of the terms involved, although it is not always in our power to reach such an analysis.[86]

The rational character of truth lies in the intelligible relation between the subject and the predicate of a proposition. It is this ideal of the reduction of all knowledge to a sequence of deductions which is expressed by Descartes's idea of a *mathesis universalis*, an idea taken over by Leibniz.

It would be interesting to observe that empiricism, as we find it in Hume, seems also to believe in the absurdity of the very idea of a truth of fact. But by putting truths of fact first, Hume realizes their unintelligibility and, far from wanting to transform the notion of truth, declares himself to be a skeptic. He thus preserves the central theses of the rationalist theory: the locus of truth is judgments, and truth consists in a tie between subject and predicate. But Hume observes that analytical logic is not sufficient to account for the relation between subject and predicate and consequently reduces the justification of judgments to a relation born from habit.

Kant has very clearly seen the difficulty inherent in the notion of truth understood as an adequation between thought and things. In the *Critique of Pure Reason*, he tries to go deeper into this definition, which in itself is but a *Namenerklärung*. Indeed, truth can never be demonstrated as the adequation between thought and things, since things can be given only in thought. "My thought must correspond to objects. But I can compare my

84. Ernst Cassirer, *Erkenntnisproblem* (Berlin: Bruno Cassirer, 1907), II, 48.
85. *Ibid.*, p. 51.
86. "Letters to A. Arnauld," in Leibniz, *Oeuvres*, II, 62; see also Couturat, *Opuscules* (Paris: Alcan, 1903), pp. 402, 513.

thought only with objects through knowing them. Diallelon." [87]

The *Critique of Pure Reason* does search for a new conception of objects that would permit the comprehension of this concept of truth. The Kantian solution consists in asserting the purely phenomenal character of the being we know. It is not a "thing in itself" whose correspondence to our knowledge can never be guaranteed, but it is constituted by our knowledge itself. Hence, the correspondence of thought with objects can reside only in thought's faithfulness to the laws of the constitution of objects in general. Knowledge is true when it corresponds to objects, but objects are real when they are constituted according to the rules which are described in the transcendental analytic and to the syntheses presented by the table of categories. "Transcendental logic is the logic of truth, since it teaches us the principles without which no object can be thought." [88] It is the understanding, the faculty of judgment, which constitutes objects in thought. "Truth and appearance are not in objects inasmuch as they are intuited, but rather in the judgments made about them inasmuch as they are thought." [89]

With this solution, the metaphysical hypothesis of preestablished harmony which presides over Leibniz's philosophy and in fact over any theory which looks to logic for a criterion of adequation between thought and things, becomes superfluous. For Kant also, it is judgment, as a synthesis of a multiplicity, which is the locus of truth. Whereas for Leibniz the criterion of truth is analytical logic, for Kant it becomes a synthetic logic which allows us to pass from one object to another without one's being contained in the other. Obviously, the sense and value of Kant's philosophy are not limited to showing us the possibility of an a priori synthesis understood as a purely logical problem. Kant explicitly criticizes those who understand judgments as mere ties between concepts,[90] yet in the *Critique of Pure Reason* he starts from the distinction between analytic and synthetic a priori judgments. This problem is meaningful only if analytic judgments, as intrinsic ties between concepts, are seen as the ideal of

---

87. Kant, *Handschriftlicher Nachlass*, 22 vols. (Berlin: G. Reimer, 1910–42), XVI, 251 (marginal notes reproduced by the Berlin Academy edition).
88. Kant, *Critique of Pure Reason* (Riga: J. F. Hartkhock, 1787), B 87.
89. *Ibid.*, B 350.
90. *Ibid.*, B 140–41.

rationality, because only then can one ask what the tie is which relates the subject and predicate of a synthetic judgment.

In any event, it is this aspect of Kantian philosophy, Kantianism as an elaboration of a synthetic logic, which leads a philosophy such as Hamelin's to a total deduction of the universe. For Hamelin, who is very much aware of these problems, all forms of empiricism are necessarily tainted with irrationality. A perfect science finds nothing given, since it deduces everything. But traditional logic is not sufficient and needs to be boosted or even replaced by a synthetic logic. By means of this synthetic logic, which moves from thesis to antithesis and synthesis, we are given the most striking example of the transformation of temporal and historical reality into a purely "mathematical" reality, in the sense that it is constructed by a deductive motion which derives, although in a synthetic manner, one concept from another.

This current of thought presupposes the idea of a subjectivity which exists independently of its objects and needs to reach them by means of spontaneous acts. This spontaneity is manifested in judgments (according to Kant, judgments constitute objects), and it is in judgments that the very origin of the phenomenon of truth lies. It is also this conception of a subject, independent of all objects (i.e., reified), which explains the very idea of the adequation of thought to things that is possible only in a homogeneous sphere. Once subjects are conceived on the model of things, one can understand perfectly how representations can be similar or dissimilar to things.

Husserl's transformation of the concept of truth is based on his concept of consciousness.

Consciousness is not a bundle of purely subjective sensations which in turn would have to represent or be equivalent to being.[91] A subject is a being which, inasmuch as it exists, is already in the presence of the world, and this is what constitutes its very being. Hence, truth cannot consist in the adequation of thought to things if this is understood as the adequation of a subjective representation and an existing object, because originally we are not directed toward our representation but are representing being. *It is in this presence of consciousness to objects that the primary phenomenon of truth lies.* What is called "adequation of thought to things" is understandable only on the basis of this primary phenomenon. As we have shown, the adequation consists in the

91. *Ideen*, § 86, p. 176.

correspondence between an object as it is thought in an act of signification with an object as it is seen intuitively. The object of both acts is the same and is on the same level of being. If a judgment may be true it is not *qua* judgment, *qua* asserting something or other, but *qua* intuition, *qua* facing its correlate, a *Sachverhalt*, in the same way that perceived things are faced by sensible intuition. Truth does not become possible with judgment; on the contrary, judgments presuppose the primary phenomenon of truth, which consists in facing being. The fact of making a judgment about an object is only a new mode of facing it.

So, for Husserl, sensibility is already capable of reason, because one may already speak of the existence or nonexistence of sensible objects. We have shown how synthetic acts and "objectivities" such as judgments are combinations, by means of categories, of those acts and objects that have only one articulation, *monothetic* acts or objects. We insisted on this in the preceding chapter by showing that the difference between judgments and "representations" is not a difference in quality but in matter. We intimated that judgments, inasmuch as they refer to objects, have a structure analogous to perception. Our analyses, whose goal was to show the formation of *Sachverhalte* in second-degree acts, have also shown us that their complexity does not in any way detract from the intuitive character of the apprehension of *Sachverhalte*. In *Ideen*,[92] besides admitting synthetic propositions such as judgments, Husserl develops the notion of a proposition's having a single articulation. Such a proposition can be justified or not, i.e., it is capable of being true or false.

Husserl's theory of intuition does not attack the value of discursive logical reasoning (whether analytic or synthetic) by opposing an intuitive method to it. His theory does not assert the need to stop somewhere in the sequence of deductions or the need to assert the existence of self-evident truths, since such an assertion would not get at the essence of truth. This assertion would still see in deduction the essential element of reason, by defining in a purely negative manner those truths that have no need to be proved. Husserl was looking for the primary phenomenon of truth and reason, and he found it in intuition, here understood as an intentionality which reaches being.[93] He found it in

---

92. *Ibid.*, § 133, p. 274.
93. *Ibid.*, § 19, p. 36; § 24, p. 44; § 76, p. 141.

"vision," the ultimate source of all reasonable assertions.[94] Vision has "justification" as its function, because it gives its object in a direct manner; inasmuch as vision realizes its object, it is reason.[95] This is why explanation and experimentation, as practiced in science, are not the only forms of rational knowledge.[96] They are determined by the essence of nature, which is their object.[97] Deduction and explanation are required by the nature of certain objects; it belongs to the essence of objects of this type that they can be only mediately revealed. Deduction is only a mediate way to reach intuition,[98] which is itself reason. "To give no value to 'I see it' as an answer to the question 'why?' would be absurd." [99]

In these last lines, we have had in mind the remarks which Pradines has devoted to Husserl's intuitive method in his book on *The Problem of Sensation*.[100] We would like to devote some time to them.

Pradines has clearly seen the essential role of intuition in conscious life and the insufficiency of the method of traditional psychology which does not take it into account. He therefore concedes to Husserl that a "sane and honest description" must constitute the starting point of the science of mind. More precisely, he wants to see in this description nothing more than a starting point. Indeed, according to Pradines, the explanation of the mystery of intuitive intention, the explanation of the tran-

94. *Ibid.*, § 136, p. 282; § 141, p. 293.
95. *Ibid.*, § 136, pp. 283 f.
96. Husserl certainly saw a problem in the relation between "explanatory" sciences and descriptive sciences; *ibid.*, § 73, p. 137.
97. *Ibid.*, § 50, p. 94.
98. *Ibid.*, § 141, pp. 293–95.
99. *Ibid.*, § 19, p. 36.
100. Maurice Pradines, *Le Problème de la sensation* (Paris: Alcan, 1928), preface, p. 11. This work is one of the first in France in which some of Husserl's theses are explicitly mentioned and discussed. It is interesting to note that it is the notion of intentionality and not the alleged "logicism" of Husserl that Pradines quite naturally attacks as being the central point of phenomenology. It is mainly —and even only—the "logicism" that has been seen by Spaier, *La Pensée concrète*; Albert Burloud, *La Pensée d'après les recherches expérimentales de H. J. Watt, Messer et Bühler* (Paris: Alcan, 1927); and even by Victor Delbos in his article "Husserl: Sa Critique du psychologisme et sa conception d'une logique pure," *Revue de métaphysique et de morale*," Vol. XIX (1911). It must be noted that Delbos's article precedes the publication of *Ideen* (1913). See also René Kremer, *Le Néo-Réalisme américain* (Louvain-Paris: Alcan, 1920), pp. 290, 295.

scendence of consciousness with respect to itself, must still be made once this transcendence has been described. Pradines believes that intuition will need another method if it does not want to present its assertions as mere beliefs, in the manner of Thomas Reid. This is how he tries to clarify the role of the "phenomenological reduction," whose place in Husserl's system we shall see later.[101] For Pradines, the reduction consists in not accepting the spontaneous assertions of consciousness through a sort of prudence "reminiscent of the Cartesian doubt."

The difficulties which Pradines sees in intuition, which is incapable of explaining "the enigma" of its own transcendence, do not concern the intentional character of consciousness. Intentionality for Pradines is not only the essence of consciousness; it is, so to speak, its very definition.

What Pradines objects to in Husserl must certainly be found elsewhere. It is in its implied realism that the transcendence of consciousness with respect to itself would be an enigma. How can we have faith in an intuition which claims to reach being, a being which in the realist hypothesis exists for itself? How, when we describe the intuitive data, can we go beyond the stage of "descriptive psychology" and obtain ontological assertions? In this form, the objection is not without importance. But we ourselves have presented it in this form. In order to answer the objections, we have dwelt on Husserl's notion of being, to which we shall return presently. We have seen that the notion of being was identified with the notion of "intentional" or "experienced" object. We have shown,[102] and shall again,[103] that the realism of the *Logische Untersuchungen* was only a stage in the elaboration of phenomenology, and that what is now called the idealism of *Ideen* had to appear in order to give an ontological value to the data of intuition. The idealism of *Ideen* is an intentional idealism and consequently conceives in a new way the mode of existing and the structure of consciousness, as well as the "phenomenal" existence of things. This idealism seems to solve the "enigma of intuition."

It is also because intentional idealism is Husserl's essential attitude that the phenomenological reduction cannot be a simple prudential measure, dictated by caution, with respect to the transcendent assertions of consciousness. It is rather the pas-

101. See below, chap. 7, pp. 146 ff.
102. See above, chaps. 1 and 2.
103. See below, chap. 6.

sage to an absolute viewpoint [104] from which the world is considered *qua* constituted by the intentions of consciousness. Despite their analogy, Husserl explicitly distinguishes the reduction from the Cartesian doubt.[105] The reduction neither undermines nor doubts the truths of intuition.

Finally, as far as we are concerned here, Husserl's intuitionism could have been assimilated to that of Reid, as proposed by Pradines, and could have "justified any mysticism," if it had been asserting the existence of some indisputable principles inherent to consciousness through some sort of "natural magics." However, there is nothing magical about Husserl's intuitionism. It is the result of the analysis of the primary phenomenon of truth, analysis which finds intuition to be a part of every form of reason. In other words, intuition, as Husserl understands it, is not a mode of immediate knowledge which can be put beside other modes while judgments were made about the scope and value of this immediate knowledge compared with mediated knowledge. Intuition, for Husserl, is the very course of thought toward truth, the course which is at the basis of anything that could be used to justify intuition itself.

The transformation of the notion of truth is accompanied by a similar revolution in the notion of being, and we find here again the conclusions of our first chapters. Being is nothing other than the correlate of our intuitive life,[106] because the latter does not aim at representations but always at being. This thesis is obviously directed against any realism or idealism which admits to a thing in itself behind the phenomena. It is also directed against naïve realism, which attributes to what is given a "mythological" existence. In chapter 2 [107] we have tried to show the absurdity of this conception. Moreover, the thesis that being is nothing other than the correlate of intuition is also directed against a more radical form of idealism, one which sees in transcendent being a construction of the mind, the latter being independent of the former. The correlation with consciousness which makes up the very being of the world does not mean that the world is merely a construction of a subject following the rules of (analytic or synthetic) logic. It does not mean that real-

104. See below, chap. 7, p. 149.
105. See *ibid.*, p. 147 and n. 155.
106. *Ideen*, § 142, p. 296.
107. "An absolute reality is as valid an idea as a round square" (*ibid.*, § 55, p. 106). *Reality* means here "existence of a *res*."

ity or unreality depends on the correspondence or noncorrespondence to these rules. The transcendence of objects with respect to consciousness—this transcendence as such—is something irreducible to a construction by means of categories, and it cannot be resolved into relations. In other words, the *existence* of the world cannot be reduced to the categories which form its *essence* but lies in the fact of being, so to speak, met by consciousness. Because consciousness is essentially in contact with objects, the synthesis and constitution of objects by means of categories are possible. The spontaneity of the mind, i.e., judgment, does not create objects; it is itself intelligible and possible only on the basis of intentionality, on the basis of the primary presence of consciousness to the world.[108]

It is now time to remember the conclusions of our first two chapters. We have tried to show how, for Husserl, the origin of being must be found in the intrinsic meaning of *Erlebnisse.* Having followed the analysis of the intrinsic intention of intuitive acts where being appears as the correlate of such acts, we are in a position to believe Husserl's thesis and to look for the origin of the notion of being in acts of intuition, without having to wonder whether the objects of intuition conform to the model of being that we have in mind. As long as the notion of being is not bound to that of experience, as it is in Husserl's *Ideen,* one cannot, in the theory of intuition, go beyond the stage of a "descriptive psychology." In *Ideen,* Husserl has seen that psychology, understood in a certain way, is closely related to philosophy itself.[109] This does not mean that Husserl reduces philosophy to a naturalistic psychology, but rather that he is inventing a new psychology, a phenomenological psychology.[110] The phenomenological reduction is *the purification of concrete life from any naturalistic interpretation of its existence* [111] yet also the awareness of the fact that the origin of being is in the concrete life of consciousness. This is the reason that Husserl justifiably sees the keystone of his system, the very beginning of phenomenology, in the phenomenological reduction.

It is in intuitive life that we must look for the origin of being, and the concept of intuition is wide enough to account for all

---

108. See above, pp. 80, 88.
109. See also *Phil. als str. Wiss.,* p. 302 [p. 91], and *passim.*
110. *Ideen,* introduction, p. 2.
111. *Ibid.,* p. 4; § 76, pp. 141–42.

the forms of being and to respect the originality of each.[112] We have already shown how the objects of judgments, the *Sachverhalte*, have a mode of existence different from that of the objects of sensible perception. We should also note the different manner of existing demonstrated by material and psychological objects, by ideal and individual objects, by the objects of physics and those of everyday life.[113] These differences are exactly why we may begin to see a new dimension in the study of being, the very dimension which Husserl accuses modern philosophy of ignoring.[114] Rather than directing ourselves toward an existing *objectivity*, we can direct our intuition toward existence itself and all the originality of its structure. Rather than retaining the attitude of the sciences, which do not wonder what the objectivity of objects means but presuppose this objectivity without clarifying it, philosophy is concerned with knowing which is the particular mode of being transcendent, of being given to consciousness,[115] which is proper to each region of objects. This is the problem of philosophical intuition which will be examined in our last chapter.

Let us indicate at once—albeit briefly, because the interest of this remark can be fully grasped only in the context of the problems raised in the last chapter—that although intuition appears as a very broad notion which makes no presuppositions about the mode of existence of its object, one should not forget that, for Husserl, intuition is a theoretical act, and that inasmuch as other acts can reach being they must, according to the *Logische Untersuchungen*, be based on a representation. We have studied this question at length in the last chapter. If *Ideen* modifies, with respect to the *Logische Untersuchungen*, the thesis according to which representation is the basis of all acts, it does not modify it enough to forbid us to say that each position of being (thesis) includes a representative thesis. We must, therefore, observe first that, for Husserl, being is correlative to theoretical intuitive life, to the evidence of an *objectifying act*. This is why the Husserlian concept of intuition is tainted with intellectualism and is possibly too narrow. None of Husserl's attempts to introduce into the constitution of being categories which do not come from theoretical life succeeds in suppressing the primacy or the universality of the theoretical attitude. The characters of usage,

112. *Ibid.*, § 20, p. 38.
113. *Ibid.*, § 21, p. 39.
114. *Phil. als str. Wiss.*, pp. 289–90 [pp. 71–72].
115. *Ideen*, § 87, p. 180.

value, etc., can exist only as grafted on a being that is the correlate of a representation.

This certainly does not mean that we find an absolute logicism in Husserl. Yet this part of his philosophy, logicism and the theory of the *Wesensschau* (intuition of essences), is universally known and almost popular (at least by name). A great number of philosophers even believe that they have found here the very meaning of Husserl's theory. We must devote a special chapter to this aspect of phenomenology, which, in reality, expresses the attitude of only the first volume of the *Logische Untersuchungen* taken in isolation. We shall try to establish that the genuine meaning of Husserl's logicism and of his *Wesensschau* can be understood only on the basis of the theses which we have just discussed, and that both logicism and the *Wesensschau* are, in his system, consequences of the points which we made when we saw the source of existence in the intrinsic meaning of life.

6 / The Intuition of Essences

THE *Logische Untersuchungen* (particularly the first volume) has earned Husserl the reputation of being a logicist and a "Platonic realist."

The *Logische Untersuchungen* begins with a critique of psychologism in logic. Volume I is directed against the identification of logical laws with psychological laws.[1]

However, the psychology which Husserl attacks in logic is a naturalistic psychology, one understood as a science of facts, like all natural sciences. He conceives it as follows: "However the latter discipline may be defined . . . it is universally agreed that psychology is a factual and therefore an empirical science."[2] The laws toward which such a psychology tends are only "approximate regularities of coexistence and succession."[3] Derived by induction, these laws are a posteriori, contingent, and merely probable.

This last point is important and has not always been emphasized. When Husserl pleads for a divorce between logic and psychology, he is talking about naturalistic psychology. Hence such a separation need not be imposed upon any psychology whatsoever.[4]

1. See Victor Delbos, "Husserl: Sa Critique du psychologisme et sa conception d'une logique pure," *Revue de métaphysique et de morale*, Vol. XIX (1911).
2. *LU*, I, 60–61 [p. 98].
3. *Ibid.*, p. 62 [p. 98].
4. See below, chap. 7, where we show the relation between psychology and phenomenology.

In any event, Husserl asserts the independence of logic with respect to naturalistic psychology. He shows that the laws which govern logical relations are, by their very meaning, exact and a priori and hence specifically different from psychological laws. Yet he also shows that, by virtue of its very meaning, logic does not presuppose psychology and is independent of it.

> No logical law implies a *matter of fact*, not even the existence of presentations or judgments or other phenomena of knowledge. No logical law, properly understood, is a law for the facticities of mental life, and so not a law for presentations (as experiences), nor for judgments (experiences of judging), nor finally for our other mental experiences.[5]

From there follows the assertion, repeated in *Ideen*,[6] that logical laws have the same validity whether they be known or not.

In the second stage of his critique, Husserl shows the absurd consequences of identifying logical and psychological laws: the ideality of logic, or its ideal existence, is the very condition of truth. If one reduces logical laws to generalizations based on a logical experience which is understood as an experience of nature, then one must refuse them any character of necessity and fall into absolute skepticism, i.e., into absurdity, because absolute skepticism is self-contradictory.[7]

In the third stage, Husserl tries to uncover some mistakes involved in the principles of psychologism, namely, the ignorance of the intentional character of consciousness and the misconceptions about the fact that the objects of logic, which are ideal objects, are transcendent with respect to the psychological acts in which they are thought.[8] (This is another way of asserting the independent existence of logical objects with respect to consciousness.)

The second volume of the *Logische Untersuchungen* takes up these theses again. The second investigation establishes the irreducible character of *ideas to facts* and criticizes in detail the theories of the British empiricists, conceptualists, and nominalists, which try to reduce one to the other. The third and fourth investigations deal with ideal laws which have their source in "essences."

5. *LU*, I, 69 [p. 104].
6. *Ideen*, § 22, p. 42.
7. *LU*, I, 32 ff. [pp. 76 ff.]; *Ideen*, § 20, p. 37.
8. See also *Ideen*, § 23, pp. 42–43.

From these passages emerges the idea of a pure logic and of a science of pure essences which seem to be completely independent of naturalistic psychology.

The ideal world is rehabilitated. Logical relations are submitted to an autonomous set of laws. They constitute the world of pure forms that is discovered by formalization [9] and provides the object of the *mathesis universalis* of which traditional logic and algebra are only branches.[10] These theses are reminiscent of those of British logicism. Beside the world of forms, there is a world of material (*sachhaltig*) essences that appears in generalizations: the essence of red, of being colored, of man, of society, etc. These essences constitute the foundation of the necessary truths which we grasp in them through Platonic contemplation. Such are the truths of geometry which study the essence of space and such truths as: "every color is extended," "every sound has a certain volume," etc. The field of necessary truths encompasses the universe of essences, which is unlimited and of which traditional philosophy has not even guessed the extent. This is one way of understanding Husserl's philosophy. According to this interpretation, which is current not only outside of Germany [11] but also often in Germany, the meaning of Husserl's philosophy would be a possibly impoverished but newly found Platonic realism. It is a realism of ideas in perfect accordance with a general realism, since the *Logische Untersuchungen* defends the transcendence of material things with respect to consciousness as well as the transcendence of the ideal world.

The first volume of the *Logische Untersuchungen* in particular (especially after a superficial reading), and attaching an excessive importance to the second, third, and fourth investigations, have led to the belief that the essence of Husserl's philosophy is logicism and Platonism. In the fifth and sixth investigations, Husserl turns back *toward consciousness* in order to determine the essence of representation, truth, object, and evidence. These investigations were published at the same time as the others and could have permitted this misunderstanding to be avoided, but they were read less and badly understood, so they appeared to indicate a return by Husserl toward the psychologism which he had

9. See above, pp. 75–78.
10. *LU,* I, 227 [p. 225]. Concerning the resemblance between Husserl's pure logic and Anglo-Saxon logicism, see René Kremer: *Le Néo-Réalisme américain* (Louvain-Paris: Alcan, 1920), pp. 290–94.
11. Delbos himself seems to accept it.

so strongly fought.[12] These circumstances explain the surprise caused by the *transcendental idealism* of *Ideen.*

In opposition to this misconception, we want to emphasize that what is called "Husserl's Platonic realism" (an expression which Husserl explicitly rejects) [13] is based on the transcendental idealism of *Ideen* as we have tried to understand it.

First, in Volume I of the *Logische Untersuchungen* what is denied is not any relation of logic to consciousness but rather one definite relation, that which is assumed by psychologism.

Indeed, the real problem raised by the Prolegomena is that of determining whether the study of consciousness, understood as psychology, can furnish the theoretical science on which logic, understood as the normative science of thought, should be based. Through studying the logical activity in which the very being of logic can be found, Husserl asserts the originality of logic and its irreducibility to psychology. Given the original problem, it follows that logic is in no way a science of subjectivity. Its relation to psychology is not that of a normative to a theoretical science. Yet the fact that neither psychology nor, more generally, any science of subjectivity can serve as a foundation for logic must be understood in a very precise sense. Psychology is not a science capable, in this particular case, of giving a basis to the normative science of logic. However, this does not preclude the existence of a necessary relation between the object of logic and subjectivity. On the contrary, Husserl is far from separating logic and subjectivity. Truth is to be found neither among psychologists nor among their adversaries, but in between.[14] "The argument only proves one thing, that psychology *helps* in the foundation of logic, not that it has the only or the main part in this, not that it provides logic's essential foundation in the sense above defined (§ 16)." [15] Husserl admits, agreeing with the psychologists, the existence of a relation between the two sciences. Let us remember, however, that psychology in Husserl's day was naturalistic and conceived conscious life in the form of psychic contents.[16] How can we then understand that the objects of logic can be related to subjects and yet manifest a lawfulness inde-

12. *LU*, III, vi [p. 663].
13. *Ideen,* § 22, p. 40.
14. *LU*, I, 58 [p. 96].
15. *Ibid.,* p. 59 [p. 96].
16. See above, chap. 1.

pendent from subjects? Only the idea of intentionality can make this intelligible.

In summary, we can say that, as far as naturalistic psychology is concerned, its divorce from logic is complete and final. Psychology is not the theoretical science which founds the normative science of logic. However, one cannot separate the philosophical study of logic from the study of subjectivity understood in a different manner. One may say that Volume I of the *Logische Untersuchungen,* in order to give a philosophical foundation to logic, attacks a bad psychology, and that Volume II searches for a good one. Husserl realizes that to psychologize essences falsifies not only the sense of essences but also the sense of pychology.[17]

Furthermore, not only does Volume I of the *Logische Untersuchungen* not separate logic from life; the argument of the whole book is based on the conviction that the origin of being is in life and that being conforms to the intrinsic meaning of conscious life.

Indeed, at each step of his argument, Husserl appeals to the intrinsic meaning of consciousness. He does not begin with a definition of what is logical and what is ideal; he takes the objects of logic as they occur in the part of life which deals with logic. He appeals to the meaning that logical laws have as parts of our own life. As he uncovers the prejudices of psychologism, he again analyzes the intrinsic meaning of logical life in order to show that objects are given as transcendent to the acts in which they are thought, and that evidence is not a feeling but a direct vision of objects. The same attitude is present in Husserl's assertion of the irreducible character of general and ideal objects. There are ideal specific objects which are absolutely irreducible to individual objects, because there is a form of consciousness of which the intrinsic, irreducible meaning is to give them as such.[18]

> The generality of meanings . . . is something *felt* as immanent *in each individual case* where a general name is understood. . . . A new type of reference makes its appearance, in which we . . . [do not] mean the intuitively apparent object . . . but the quality or form exemplified in the latter, which we understand in general fashion, as a unity in the sense of a species.[19]

17. *Ideen,* § 61, p. 116.
18. *LU,* II, 122, 171–72 ff. [pp. 350, 390 ff.]; *Ideen,* § 25, P. 45.
19. *LU,* II, 187 [pp. 403–4].

The existence of ideal objects means nothing other than that our concrete life can be directed at ideal objects; [20] we value them as real, we identify them, and consequently we can compare them with each other. They can be subjects of numerous predicates; they can be collected, numbered, etc.[21] General, ideal objects are, in one word, given. Propositions and judgments, as they appear in our life, may have subjects and attributes that are general.[22] It is because of the intrinsic intention of ideative life that Husserl condemns empiricism's pretension to reduce general to individual objects—whether such an attempt can succeed or not.[23]

Husserl is perfectly aware of the impact of his argument. Introducing Volume II of the *Logische Untersuchungen,* he declares that, to uncover logical notions, one should go beyond the meaning of words, which are always ambiguous; one must grasp the phenomena in question at their origin in conscious life, whose activity is a theoretical activity. It is reasonable to think that this assertion expresses more than a simple precaution of logical method and contains the germ of the deeply philosophical principle which emerges in *Ideen,* i.e., the very principle of phenomenology. In logic, the philosophical attitude consists in a reflection on the naïve life of the logicians, who are themselves only directed toward their objects. This was already intimated in § 71 of Volume I of the *Logische Untersuchungen.*[24]

The theory of being in *Ideen* brings the last justification to this method; the notion of being is so closely related to that of *experience* that we may grant philosophical value to the data of reflection, even though they seem to be purely psychological. We are justified in making judgments that have ontological value. It is only then that we can be sure that in reflection we have, not a mere representation of being (which may be inadequate), but being itself. It is only then that we may speak of the *existence* of ideal objects as being, for instance, irreducible to individual objects, as opposed to speaking merely of the irreducibility of the *consciousness* of ideal objects to the *consciousness* of individual objects. Of course transcendental idealism, as we described it in chapter 2, is not yet aware of itself in the *Logische Untersuchungen,* and there are even several passages which seem to go against

20. *Ideen,* § 22, p. 41.
21. *LU,* II, 111–12 [p. 342].
22. *Ibid.*
23. *Ibid.,* p. 156 [p. 378]; see also *Ideen,* § 19, p. 36.
24. *LU,* I, 253–54 [pp. 243–44].

our interpretation. We do not want to deny that there is an evolution from the *Logische Untersuchungen* to *Ideen;* Husserl himself admits this.[25] But for Husserl, this evolution has mainly consisted in becoming aware of all the requirements of the thesis of the *Logische Untersuchungen* and making them explicit.[26] Husserl realizes that some parts of the *Logische Untersuchungen* form a transition to, and clearly break the ground for, the *Ideen*.[27] The course of Husserl's research is a climb in which each discovery becomes, as one gets higher, inserted in a more complete whole, in a larger horizon. Moreover, even if there is in the *Logische Untersuchungen* a certain hesitation between realism and idealism, it is clear that, inasmuch as the realistic aspect prevails, the work does not go beyond the point of view of a "descriptive psychology."

We can summarize by saying that Husserl can overcome psychologism and assert the objectivity of logic only by taking into consideration the intrinsic meaning of life, which is directed at logical phenomena and ideal objects. It is only the Husserlian notion of existence with its correlation with experience which gives to those phenomena status as being.

Husserl's "logicism" is not the assertion of the independence of logic with respect to psychology, of the ideal with respect to subjectivity. His "Platonic idealism," the rehabilitation of the world of essences and of logical categories, has its roots in the theory of the absolute existence of consciousness that we have tried to explain in chapter 2. This is how the unity of the phenomenological inspiration is manifested: the so-called "Platonic realism" and the so-called "logicism" are only its consequences. Husserl's notion of existence goes beyond a naturalistic ontology for which all existence is an empirical existence individuated in time.[28] This allows us to say that essences, and the ideal world in general, exist.

What meaning should we then give to the existence of essences?

As we have shown, essences exist differently than individual objects. They are neither spatial nor temporal, so that they neither emerge nor disappear.[29] In this resides their ideality. This

---

25. See *Ideen*, § 61, p. 117.
26. *Ibid.*, introduction, p. 2.
27. *Ibid.*, § 61, p. 117.
28. *LU*, II, 125 [p. 353].
29. *Ibid.*, pp. 124, 155 [pp. 352, 377].

ideality of essences and general objects is neither negligible nor indeterminate but rather admits of subdivisions and descriptive differences; [30] the generality of the form "an A" is different from that of "all As" or from that of "A in general." It is by reflecting on ideative life, by paying attention to its intrinsic meaning, that one can touch, so to speak, not only the ideality of essences but also the various forms of their ideality. We can mention here only all the forms of the ideality of essences and of general objects that Husserl's analyses carefully distinguish. This ideality is not, from Husserl's point of view, a genuine predicate or determination (as is, for instance, the property of being extended); it is primarily a different mode of existing. It reveals a new dimension of being. The ideality of an object does not mean that it first exists and then is characterized by its indifference with respect to space and time. Their indifference, etc., constitute the very mode of existing of ideal objects—their mode of being given to consciousness and of being *constituted* there, as Husserl would say. As Hering so aptly remarks, "It is not *qua* 'general' but *qua* ideal that [general ideas] do not belong to this world." [31]

One can thereby understand what is the very principle of the criticism which Husserl, in the second investigation, directs against British empiricism's attempt to reduce the ideality of essences to a property of individual objects. When Locke tried to explain generality by means of indeterminate individuals, he was mistaken from the beginning, even if we ignore the impossibility of such a reduction, because he was neglecting the ideal mode of existence of general objects. [32] We would commit the same fundamental mistake if we tried to identify essences with a character or moment of individual objects that has been isolated by an effort of attention. The genus *red* is not the red of an individual object placed in evidence, because this remains something individual, while the genus is ideal. [33] It is for the same reason that the theory of generic images has to be rejected. Generic images are vague and changing but do not thereby cease to be individual. The essence is not necessarily imprecise but can be in its own way quite determinate. Ideality is not the

30. *Ibid.*, pp. 147 (§ 16), 187, 223 [pp. 371, 404, 432].
31. Jean Hering, *Phénoménologie et philosophie religieuse* (Paris: Alcan, 1925), p. 46.
32. *LU*, II, second investigation, pp. 106–224 [pp. 335–432].
33. *Ibid.*, pp. 106–7 [p. 337].

indetermination of an object; ideality characterizes the object's mode of existing.

Such are the right to exist and the specific mode of existing of ideal objects. We can now understand what is meant by the intuition of ideal objects, the intuition of essences or *Eide*, i.e., the *eidetic intuition* or Husserl's famous *Wesensschau*.

Just like individual objects, ideal beings and essences admit of truth and falsity. Essences are not fictions about which one may say anything.[34] In geometry, for instance, one can distinguish a true from a false proposition.[35] We may have concepts which refer to essences that are "merely meant" but do not exist, as, for example, that of a regular decahedron.

In the field of essences, one can distinguish between "merely signifying" thoughts and acts that tend directly toward essences which, so to speak, possess them originally.

This act of original intuition, both in the realm of essences and in that of forms, is identified, in the *Logische Untersuchungen*, with perception, inasmuch as it belongs to the essence of perceptive activity to be paralleled by acts of imagination. Husserl broadens the notion of imagination to allow for the existence of a categorial imagination,[36] and even gives examples of it.[37]

However, in the *Vorlesungen zur Phänomenologie des inneren Zeitbewusstseins* (dated 1905–10), Husserl denies that ideal objects can be divided into perceived and imagined objects.[38] The parallel between perception and imagination is due to the temporal character of some objects.[39] The notion of intuition is more general and does not presuppose this parallelism. What applies to sensible intuition *qua* sensible does not apply to *eidetic* intuition. Here, as always, intuition is the mode of life in which the object aimed at is not only "meant" but given "in person." [40] Knowledge of ideal objects need not, like sensible perception,[41]

34. *Ibid.*, pp. 124–25 [pp. 352–53].
35. *Ideen*, § 23, p. 43; *Phil. als str. Wiss.*, p. 316 [p. 112].
36. *LU*, III, 144 [p. 786].
37. *Ibid.*, pp. 163–64 [pp. 801–2].
38. *Zeitbewusstsein*, p. 448 [p. 125].
39. In any event, intuition remains analogous to perception, inasmuch as it presents an essence "in person," inasmuch as it is susceptible of truth (*Ideen*, § 23, p. 43).
40. *Ibid.*, § 3, p. 11; *Phil. als str. Wiss.*, p. 318 [p. 115], and *passim*.
41. See above, pp. 83.

be a simple operation in order to be characterized as intuition; it is enough that it has its object given in front of it.[42]

We have already encountered the intuition of ideal objects in the form of a categorial intuition. But categories were purely formal objects. They must be distinguished from material (*sachhaltige*) essences, which constitute another type of ideal object. Such are the essences of red, triangle,[43] man, etc., or, in the field of consciousness, the essences of memory, intentionality, etc. We have shown how the intuition of formal categories is accomplished with the help of the intuition of sensible objects, and how sensible objects participate in some fashion in the constitution of a *Sachverhalt*. However, the act of *ideation* which leads to the intuition of material essences has a different structure. Of course, I must take as a starting point an individual object, for example, the red of this fabric in front of me. But what I am looking at is not an individual object but red in general, of which the individual red is but an instance. I totally abandon the intention directed at the sensible object in order to think of an ideal object. This thought may very well be an intuition, since an ideal object, considered in its instance, may be given "in person."

> We do not think of it merely in significative fashion as when we merely understand general names, but we apprehend it, *behold* it. Talk of an *intuition* . . . of the universal is in this case, therefore, well justified.[44]

Individual objects do not enter into the constitution of ideal objects, although they do enter in the case of a categorial intuition.[45] However, some relation to an individual object is necessary, and an individual object which functions as an example is a necessary element of an eidetic intuition. In the intuition of a *Sachverhalt*, the sensible objects which enter into its constitution are indispensable, since they serve as a basis for a "categorial synthesis"; similarly, individual objects are an indispensable basis for the perception of essences. The mode of existence of ideal objects in some way refers us back to individual objects and contains an implicit relation to individual objects. But the existence of individual objects does not serve as a premise for eidetic knowl-

42. On the intuition of essences, see below, chap. 7.
43. Space is not something formal like the category "object in general." There is a distinction to be made between formal mathematics, *mathesis universalis*, and material mathematics or geometry.
44. *LU*, III, 162–63 [p. 800].
45. *Ibid.*, p. 162 [p. 800].

edge, which is independent of the effective existence of individual objects.[46]

The problem of a priori knowledge touches directly upon the question of the existence of ideal objects and of the intuition of essences. In the intuitionist theory of truth, what meaning can the concept of a priori truth have? Does not the theory of intuition reduce all truths to truths of fact, since, according to this conception, truth seems to be justified by experience—even though experience is understood here in a broader sense than sensible experience?

We must say first that the a priori has a place in the intuition of ideal objects and in the judgments based on those objects.[47] Eidetic intuition has, in fact, a special status. Let us consider this point at greater length.

We have noticed that the realm of general objects includes objects that have different types of generality. For example, a general intention is present in all words, even when the words refer to individual objects. This special form of generality, which belongs to all expressions, confers to words the character of *concepts* and must be distinguished from the form of generality of general objects properly speaking,[48] such as the "white," "man in general," etc. Once expressed, such objects have two different characters of generality, their own and that of the expression. But even inside the sphere of general objects proper, one must introduce a distinction separating general objects in general from *pure essences.*

In the *Logische Untersuchungen,* this distinction is not made. In *Ideen,* it is not made explicitly, although it is of capital importance. In the *Logische Untersuchungen,* Husserl identifies a priori knowledge with the intuition of pure essences. But as long as there is no distinction between general objects and pure essences, one can object that the intuition of pure essences is but a hypostasis of empirical experience, since there are general objects which have a purely inductive origin.[49] One can raise the

---

46. *Ideen,* § 4, p. 13; § 6, pp. 16–17; § 34, p. 60; *Phil. als str. Wiss.,* p. 316 [p. 112].

47. See, for example, *Phil. als str. Wiss.,* p. 322 [p. 121].

48. *Ideen,* § 124, pp. 257, 259; § 94, p. 194; *LU,* III, 102–3 [pp. 331–32]. Concerning the distinction between "concept" and "essence," see *Ideen,* § 10, p. 23.

49. See Reinhard Kynast, *Das Problem der Phänomenologie* (Breslau: Trewendt & Granier, 1917), and *Intuitive Erkenntnis* (Breslau: Trewendt & Granier, 1919).

following objection to Husserl: "If you have the concept of a swan in general, you could say 'all swans are white,' and claim that this is a truth based on the intuition of the essence of swans. But your concept of swan comes only from induction, and your alleged intuition of the essence of swans may be false. There are indeed black swans." Hence, if there is no distinction between "ideal objects" and "pure essences," the truths revealed by the intuition of essences are either mere tautology (in the essence of "white swan there is whiteness") or they include inductive truths.

But if we consider this a valid objection, we are attributing an absurdity to Husserl, or at best a philosophical naïveté which could never have been his. We must admit that the distinction has never been made in the published works of Husserl,[50] and we do not know the characteristics by which the intuition of pure essences differ from the intuition of other general objects. The description of eidetic intuition which we have summarized hardly goes beyond the very general phenomenon of the intuition of ideal objects. How could the objects of ideal intuition be, by virtue of the internal structure of this intuition, pure essences? We cannot clarify this problem by means of the texts we have. We can, however, understand the remarkable efforts in this direction which were made by some of Husserl's students.[51] In particular, Hering has the merit of having raised this problem and of having distinguished empirical and a priori essences.

However, Husserl makes this distinction, at least implicitly. Certainly what he means by essence, as the foundation of a priori law, is not merely any general idea. On page nine of *Ideen,* when he tries to characterize essences, he says: "An individual object is not just an individual, a *'Dies da!'* that happens once [*einmaliger*]. It possesses, inasmuch as it is 'in itself' constituted in such or such a way, its own nature, as well as a set of predicates [*Prädikabilien*] which must belong to it in order

50. We believe that the unpublished works try to justify this distinction.

51. See, in particular, "Idee, Wesen, Wesenheit," *Jahrbuch für Philosophie und phänomenologische Forschung,* IV (1921), 495 ff., and *Phénoménologie et philosophie religieuse,* p. 52. See also Hans Lipps, *Untersuchungen zur Phänomenologie der Erkenntnis,* Vols. I and II (Bonn: F. Cohen, 1927–28); and Roman Ingarden, "Essentiale Fragen," *Jahrbuch für Philosophie und phänomenologische Forschung,* VI (1923).

for other relative, secondary determinations to be able to be attributed to it." In order to characterize the essence of an object, Husserl does not limit himself to discussing its ideality, he does not simply oppose it to the individual *"Dies da";* it is not enough for him to raise an individual object, with all its determination, to a generality, to the ideal level, in order to make it into an essence.[52] In the determination of objects there is a hierarchy, and some objects are required for others to be possible. The essence of an object is its necessary structure:[53] what makes it what it is, what makes any of its empirical characterizations a priori possible and comprehensible, or, in short, its principle.

For instance, in order to have a determinate intensity, tone, and pitch, a sound must have tone, intensity, and pitch in general. They are a set of mutually and necessarily related characteristics which constitute the necessary structure of sounds.

What is the meaning of the necessity proper to the structure of objects? What is the meaning of the necessity which is inherent in the laws founded on essences? These questions are directly related to the role of intuition. Indeed, given that an act of intuition is always an act of reason, what is the meaning of the necessity proper to laws founded on essences? Is not the problem of the nature of reason, as expressed in the following question, totally unresolved? How are we to understand and explain the necessity of truths based on essences? Are we not led to look for the *reason* for this necessity? Should we not see the fundamental act of reason in those discursive steps through which thought deduces the necessity of essences?

To answer these questions, we must return to the notion of eidetic necessity as it is elaborated in the third and fourth investigations. We shall then see that essential necessity owes nothing to deduction, since deduction itself is but a particular case of the essential necessity which is the prime aspect and the very model of rational necessity. Furthermore, we shall be able to characterize this necessity in a positive way.

The third investigation begins by distinguishing between *dependent* and *independent contents.* To exist, dependent contents

---

52. It is in the light of this notion of essence that we must interpret the passages in which essences seem to be identified with an "idealized" *Was* (see, e.g., *Ideen,* § 3, p. 10). This "idealization" must be understood as *passage* to the necessary constitution.

53. *Ideen,* § 2, p. 9.

need other contents.[54] Color, for example, can only be extended. A house and a tree, on the contrary, are independent, since they do not need to be completed by other objects in order to exist.

What does this dependence mean?

Let us first note that "dependent content" does not mean "a content which cannot be represented without others": dependency is a character of the content itself. Being, dependent or not, is not a "subjective necessity, i.e. . . . the subjective incapacity-to-represent-things otherwise, but . . . the objectively ideal necessity of an inability-to-be-otherwise." [55]

However, if this dependency is necessarily inherent in the nature of the objects considered, then the necessity—by virtue of which color, for example, is not conceivable without extension or without a colored material object—is not purely empirical; it is not the result of induction, as the necessity of natural laws is.[56] It is based not on empirical observations (for example, at some moment of time a color seems to be extended) but on the genus, on the essence of color itself.

The necessary character of dependency is neither empirical nor logical. Logic is the science of the forms of objects in general.[57] Logical necessity is founded on the laws of logic but, precisely for that reason, it has no grip on the material content of objects. But the laws of "dependency" are "material laws." We are faced here with a form of necessity which is independent of logic [58] and of any deduction, and which has its foundation in "the specific essence of the contents, on their peculiar nature." [59] The genera and species which may serve as such foundations form the world of essences. In intuiting them, we are able to know the necessities which they impose by reason of their very nature without our having to go back to any premises and without our having to justify them by a deduction.

The intuition of material essences, such as "house," "tree," "color," "tone," "space," "sensation," and "feeling," [60] enables us to have a knowledge which is both necessary and material. For Husserl, direct vision of the necessary structure of essences seems

54. *Ibid.*, § 14, pp. 28–29.
55. *LU*, II, 239 [p. 446].
56. *Ibid.*, p. 234 [p. 441].
57. See above, p. 4, and *passim*.
58. *Ideen*, § 16, p. 31.
59. *LU*, II, 251–52 [p. 455].
60. *Ibid.*, p. 252 [p. 455].

to be the primary phenomenon of intellection.[61] Moreover, when we identify intuitive acts and acts of reason in this way, when we assert that they are neutral with respect to logic and deduction, we do not undermine the possibility of necessary knowledge; on the contrary, we provide the means to extend it to an infinite section of the matter of knowledge.

Furthermore, the necessity of the laws of deduction themselves is founded on the intuition of essences. The necessity of the conclusion of a syllogism is founded on the formal essence of its premises, in which this necessity is grasped with evidence. Each "link" in a deduction is an intuition of essences although, in this case, an intuition of *formal* essences. The role of deduction consists in providing evident intuition for a truth that is not evident by itself, by means of a series of steps that are themselves evident.[62] It is evidence, not deduction, which is the rational element in knowledge. Deduction is an act by means of which certain truths are reduced to the evidence of first principles. It is not characteristic of all rational knowledge but only of some definite domains of objects. Husserl calls a domain of truths that can be deduced from a finite number of axioms "a mathematical or definite multiplicity"; such are the objects of geometry, and the world of logical forms which are the objects of the *mathesis universalis*.[63] Hence it is clear that to take analytic or synthetic logic as the model of all intelligibility amounts to conceiving science on the image of mathematics and having too narrow a conception of reason. According to Hamelin, the essential function of reason is the construction of reality according to rules. Husserl's attitude is the exact opposite. It is not a dialectical construction which makes a law of essences intelligible; it is from the intelligibility of essential relations that dialectical constructions derive their intelligibility.

It is now possible to characterize positively the necessity of eidetic laws and the special status of a priori knowledge. Passages in the third investigation that we have already mentioned throw more light on the subject.

An independent content—which Husserl calls *concrete,* as

61. "Für die Frage nach ihrem Warum dem 'Ich *sehe es*' keinen Wert bemeissen wäre Widersinn" (*Ideen*, § 19, p. 36).

62. *Ibid.*, § 141, pp. 293–95; § 7, p. 17.

63. On all those problems, see *ibid.*, § 71, p. 132; § 7, p. 18; and *passim*.

opposed to dependent contents, which he calls *abstract* [64]—is neutral with respect to other contents and does not require any definite complement in order to become concrete. Some of the properties of independent objects may be separated from them. The fact that an object may be separated from related contents means that these contents can vary absolutely freely. This means that

> we can keep some content constant in idea despite boundless varia-tion—variation that is free, [i.e.] . . . *not excluded by a law rooted in the content's essence* [65]—of the content associated with it, and, in general, given with it. This means that it is unaffected by the elimination of any arrangement of compresent contents whatso-ever.[66]

For example, in our imagination we may vary without limit the shape of any material object; we may also imagine it at various times and places. Our imagination here is absolutely free; it is not limited by anything; and the object we consider remains con-crete, i.e., capable of existing. Now, if we try to imagine a ma-terial object without any shape at all, then we lose its concrete character, its capacity to exist. The essence of an independent object determines the limits between which we may vary its con-tents. A variation which steps over the limit imposed by the essence takes away from the object its concrete character, its independence, its capacity to exist. The essence of an object seems to express the conditions that must be realized to make its existence possible. The predicates of an object may vary with-out compromising its possibility to exist. Only the *essential* predi-cates may not vary. Moreover, it is only the stability of essential predicates which allows the other predicates to vary: any varia-tion presupposes something constant which makes the variation possible. We thus return to the definition of essence which we have already given, according to which essences are made up of a set of predicates that an object must have in order to have other predicates. This definition does not identify essence with quid-dity, but it shows that the essence is not the result of generalizing all the characters of an individual object—that only some of them play a privileged role: they constitute the very condition of the possibility of an object.

64. *Ibid.*, § 15, p. 29.
65. My italics.
66. *LU*, II, 235–36 [p. 443].

This reveals the special status of eidetic truths. Knowledge of essences is not only knowledge of an ideal world as juxtaposed to the empirical world. Eidetic sciences investigate a new dimension of being: the very conditions of its existence, the structure of objects without which they could not exist. In this sense, the knowledge of these sciences is a priori, because they reveal what is presupposed by all the other forms of knowledge. It is probably because the necessity of the laws of essences is the necessity of the conditions of the existence of being that Husserl calls those sciences *ontologies*. A priori knowledge does not differ from a posteriori knowledge by the mere fact of being necessary, "apodictic," [67] but it has a special *ontological status*.

We now understand the meaning, the place, and the function of a priori sciences with respect to natural sciences and sciences of fact in general. The discovery of a material a priori does not mean the reduction of all empirical truths to a priori truths. This has sometimes been demanded from Kant, and he has been criticized for not solving Hume's problem. Although Kant rationally deduces causality in general, he does not deduce each particular case of causality. A natural law is, however, the result of the intuition of individual facts. That is why it remains contingent, and its necessity is no more than probable. This is an essential characteristic of natural laws. The contingency of empirical facts is not determined by our being finite ignorant creatures; it belongs to the very essence of "facts." [68] A law of nature is essentially inductive.[69] Husserl's philosophy therefore refuses to reduce inductive laws to a priori laws; [70] it would falsify the meaning of facts to try to reduce them to a priori laws. When we say that essences are the principle of objects, we do not mean by "principle" a superior premise from which one can logically deduce the contingent properties of objects. (Was not this the desire of Leibniz and even of Hamelin?) "Principle" here means that which renders possible the existence of an object, the structure without which the object would be inconceivable.

There is an irreducible difference between the a priori and the a posteriori and between the functions each has in science. There must be a hiatus between causality in general, understood as an essential structure of being, and the contingent causal

67. Husserl introduces this term in *Ideen*, § 137, p. 285.
68. *Ibid.*, § 2, p. 9.
69. *LU*, I, 61 [p. 98].
70. *Ibid.*, pp. 255–57 [pp. 246–47]; *Ideen*, § 6, p. 16; § 58, p. 110.

relations between empirical beings; [71] they are on two different planes. Husserl criticizes the extreme naturalism of psychologism not only for conceiving consciousness after the model of nature but also for not seeing the function of a priori knowledge in the knowledge of nature itself.[72]

The body of a priori sciences, in whatever form they appear, is not a miracle of necessity in a world of universal contingency. The necessity of a priori sciences has an ontological character. It is inherent to the meaning of being *qua* being, and the laws which are marked by this necessity define the meaning of the beings to which they apply.[73] Once being has been defined by the ontological sciences, factual sciences can ask reasonable questions about it. Then, but only then, is it possible to experiment.[74] By itself, induction can generate only inductive necessity and not ontological necessity.[75] To ask inductive questions, to know what type of experience is required by a given domain of objects, we must first determine its ontological sense.[76] According to Husserl, the fact that Galileo saw the ontology of nature in the geometry and mathematics elaborated in antiquity has made possible the great progress of modern physics.[77] The great mistake of other sciences—psychology, for example—is to see, in the ontology of nature the ontology of all regions, or else to reject all ontology. It is therefore necessary, at least to contribute to the progress of sciences, to establish the ontologies of all the regions of objects.[78]

The absolute independence of philosophy with respect to science now becomes visible. Philosophy must work in a completely different sphere of experience and with completely different methods. On this depends not only the progress of the sciences but even their rationality. Indeed, if sciences want to reach absolute rationality,[79] if they want to avoid the crises in which the very meaning of what they study disappears,[80] then ontology must study the internal and a priori structure of their objects

71. *Phil. als str. Wiss.*, p. 318 [p. 116].
72. See *ibid.*, pp. 308–9 [p. 101].
73. *Ideen*, § 16, p. 31.
74. *Phil. als str. Wiss.*, p. 310 [p. 103].
75. *Ideen*, § 79, p. 159; *Phil. als str. Wiss.*, pp. 306–7, 320 [pp. 98, 118].
76. *Phil. als str. Wiss.*, pp. 307–8 [pp. 99–100].
77. *Ibid.*, p. 308 [p. 100]; *Ideen*, § 9, p. 20.
78. *Ideen*, § 9, p. 20.
79. *Ibid.*; *Phil. als str. Wiss.*, p. 321 [p. 119], and *passim*.
80. *Phil. als str. Wiss.*, pp. 306–7 [p. 98].

and clarify the essential categories which constitute them. Furthermore, as we have shown in the last chapter, the existence of the objects of science, and their mode of being present to consciousness, must also be clarified.

In relation to the theory of essences, the all-important function of concrete objects becomes apparent. Concrete objects are, as we have seen, those which include all the conditions for their existence.[81] The delineation of the various spheres of being is also made by means of the concept of concrete object. The ideal world of essences has a hierarchy of genera and species,[82] and the laws which are founded on these essences govern the corresponding domains of temporal beings which individuate these essences. Hence the classification of essences is also the delineation of different spheres of reality. But we do not reach a classification of being by means of the higher material genera.[83] The higher genera may encompass only an abstract element of objects (a dependent element), such as color, for example.[84] The various domains of being are determined on the basis of some *concrete individual notion*, for example "material object," "consciousness," or "animality." The concept of a region of being is defined by the set of higher genera, whose ultimate specifications are complementary and make possible concrete individuals.[85] Such a set of higher genera forms a "regional essence"—for example, the essence "nature." It is formed by the genera color, extension, time, causality, materiality, etc., which are necessarily bound together [86] by a necessity proper to the possible existence of an empirical object in nature. Besides this region there are others, such as animality, mankind, society, etc., and corresponding to these are *concrete* individuals.

The higher genera, whose set forms a region, are called material categories. In these categories are founded all the a priori laws which, in Kantian terms, are synthetic a priori.[87] They are opposed to laws based on the pure form of an object in general

---

81. On this subject, see the profound remarks of Aron Gurwitsch, "La Philosophie phénoménologique en Allemagne," *Revue de métaphysique et de morale*, XXXV, no. 4 (1928), *passim*.

82. *Ideen*, § 3, p. 10; § 14, p. 28.

83. A text which seems to imply this, in § 2, p. 9 of *Ideen*, is made more precise in § 16, pp. 30–31.

84. *Ibid.*, § 15, p. 30.

85. *Ibid.*, § 16, pp. 30–31; § 72, pp. 133–34.

86. *Ibid.*, § 72, p. 134.

87. *Ibid.*, § 16, p. 31.

which are universally valid, independently of the material essences of various regions. Husserl calls the latter analytic.[88]

The concept of category is not—and in this it differs from Kant's—borrowed from judgments: categories are the structure of being, not of knowledge. Hence, to make a table of categories, Husserl does not use traditional logic or the logic of the modern sciences of nature (as have the neo-Kantians); Husserl uses the different regions of concrete beings.

The whole of the a priori knowledge which is made possible by each region is called by Husserl a *regional ontology*.[89] At this time, regional ontologies are only *desiderata*.[90] Their realization has been attempted mainly by the first students of Husserl (those that go back to the time of the *Logische Untersuchungen*). A priori investigations of the ontologies of society, nature, etc., fill the first volumes of Husserl's *Jahrbuch*. Let us remember once more that, although these investigations are a priori, they are not necessarily deductive. Eidetic sciences are based on eidetic intuitions and are descriptive. Using as "an example" the world concretely given, perceived, or imagined,[91] we reach its essence and describe its necessary structure.

The attitude of looking at the world of objects, while leaving aside individual existence and considering only essences, is called, in phenomenological parlance, the *eidetic reduction*.[92] The world of individuals, both in consciousness and in nature, must be subjected to it. It is the first step toward the phenomenological attitude.

Following Bergson's critique of conceptual thought, one could think that the eidetic reduction ultimately deforms concrete reality. Is it not true that intuition, whose function is to place us immediately in the world of individuals, loses its contact with the concreteness of the world when it becomes eidetic intuition? Does not eidetic intuition freeze a fluctuating and imprecise reality and transform it into something dead and immutable? We have already shown that there is no contradiction between the intellect, which is the power of grasping what is ideal and abstract, and intuition, which is the immediate perception of

88. *Ibid.*, § 10, p. 22.
89. *Ibid.*, § 16, pp. 31–32; § 72, p. 134.
90. *Ibid.*, § 17, p. 32.
91. *Ibid.*, § 4, p. 12.
92. *Ibid.*, introduction, p. 4; see also *Phil. als str. Wiss.*, p. 318 [p. 116].

what is concrete. However, inasmuch as what is ideal is always stable and definite—while intuition, which is infinitely supple and changing, attempts to match the meanderings of concreteness—does not the contradiction reappear?

It does not. As early as the *Logische Untersuchungen*, Husserl distinguishes between ideas in the Kantian and those in the Platonic senses.[93] The latter are called *Eide* in *Ideen*.[94] *Eide* are essences of the individual objects we find around us, considered in all their concreteness. They have neither the exactness nor the perfect determination of geometric concepts. A certain imprecision is inherent to them, an imprecision for which scientists are not responsible.[95] Lack of exactness and indetermination belong to the essence of some objects.

> The spatial shape of the perceived tree as such taken precisely as a "moment" found in the relevant percept's intentional object, is no geometric shape, no ideal or exact shape in the sense of exact geometry. Just so a seen colour as such is no ideal colour.[96]

To try to express exactly the inexact data of perception is to deprive them of their life and concreteness.[97] Rough and vague notions, such as large and small, roundish and slanted, hot and cold, heavy and light, are what characterize the concrete world of perception, rather than the scientific and geometrical notions of line or circle, temperature or gravitation.[98] It is primarily through those inexact concepts that we determine the essence of the world. The world of exact scientific concepts is derivative, as we have shown.[99]

Botany and zoology are examples of empirical sciences which, because of the nature of their objects, use vague, inexact concepts.

> Perfect geometry and its perfect use in practice have no utility for a natural scientist interested in description. It cannot help him to express what he expresses so simply, comprehensibly, and ade-

93. *LU*, II, 245 [p. 450].
94. *Ideen*, introduction, p. 6.
95. *Ibid.*, § 73, p. 137.
96. *LU*, II, 245 [p. 450].
97. *Ideen*, § 75, p. 139.
98. We have allowed ourselves to reproduce these examples borrowed from a manuscript by Husserl. We take sole responsibility for them.
99. See above, chap. 1.

quately, in the words "toothed," "fluted," "lenticular," "umbellifer-ous," etc., concepts which by essence rather than accident are in-exact and nonmathematical.[100]

In addition to the inexact, purely empirical concepts, one may speak of a priori, inexact essences which express the essence of the world of individuals. "The essences which are grasped in the intuitive data by an act of direct ideation are inexact essences." [101] They express an object of intuition in all its concreteness.

> If we try to express by means of adequate concepts the things that are intuitively given with their essential intuitive characters, then we must take them as they are given. They are given as ill defined [fliessende].[102]

The world of perception becomes the object of an eidetic science. Space, time, color, and sounds can be studied in their essences. But the descriptive science of space is not geometry. The space studied by geometry is already idealized. Space as it appears in concrete life is not geometrical. It must be described by means of *morphological notions*.[103] We will not explore this last point any further, since it does not occur in the writings of Husserl that have been published so far.

Husserl's essential idea is to assert the primacy of inexact morphological essences over exact mathematical essences. This primacy can easily be explained by the fact that exact essences are only idealizations of inexact ones. The various nuances of red (inexact essences of a certain type) represent the various degrees of the ideal red which they more or less approximate. This ideal red toward which they all tend is not the genus red. With respect to the genus red, ideal red is an ideal limit. The genus remains asymptotical to the ideal. Husserl calls this sort of ideality the *Idea in the Kantian sense of the term*.[104] Ideas arise from the comparison of a series of *Eide* which tend to but never reach a limit, an ideal. From this it follows that *Eide* have a certain primacy over Ideas.[105]

100. *Ideen*, § 74, p. 138.
101. *LU*, II, 245 [p. 450].
102. *Ideen*, § 74, pp. 138, 139.
103. This is how Husserl describes inexact essences.
104. This reminds us of the determination of the notion of "Idea" by Kant in the *Critique of Pure Reason* (Riga: J. F. Hartkhoch, 1787), B 370–75. See *Ideen*, § 74, p. 138.
105. *Ideen*, § 72, p. 135; § 74, pp. 138–39. See applications of this notion of "Idea" in *ibid.*, § 83, pp. 166–67; § 143, pp. 297–98.

The distinction Husserl discovered, between morphological essences as the result of ideation and exact essences as the result of idealization, permits us to escape the dilemma raised by Bergson. An intuition may be ideative without thereby falsifying the meaning of concrete reality, as Bergson assumed it would. Although inexact essences are, like mathematical essences, the foundation of necessary laws, they nevertheless express all that is changing, continuous, and vague in reality. The conceptional essence that Bergson criticizes is a geometrical ideal which results not from *ideation* (which grasps the essence of things with all the vagueness proper to them) but from the idealization which transposes to an ideal limit the given concreteness of things. Geometrical concepts, like other scientific concepts, are the result of this idealization of concreteness, but they are not the only possible concepts.[106] Similarly, the mathematical sciences which proceed by deduction from a finite number of axioms are not the only eidetic sciences.[107] Furthermore, scientific concepts derive their origin and their meaning from the concrete world. We constantly translate idealized essences so as to understand them in the language of the concrete world.[108] Thus we should not consider the description of the *inexact* aspect of the concrete world as temporary and insufficient. On the contrary, this description will always serve as a foundation to scientific knowledge, because it is a source of principles, because it is a philosophical science. In order to respect the intrinsic meaning of our life, we must give primacy to the being of the world of perception in all its inexactitude.[109]

Here again, one can reproach Husserl for his intellectualism. Even though he attains the profound idea that, in the ontological order, the world of science is posterior to and depends on the vague and concrete world of perception, he may have been wrong in seeing the concrete world as a world of objects that are primarily perceived. Is our main attitude toward reality that of theoretical contemplation? Is not the world presented in its very being as a center of action, as a field of activity or of *care*—to speak the language of Martin Heidegger?

106. *Ibid.*, § 72, p. 133.
107. *Ibid.*, § 75, p. 141.
108. We owe this idea to a conversation with Husserl, but we take full responsibility for it.
109. *Ideen*, § 52, p. 98.

7 / Philosophical Intuition

THE INTUITION we have discussed so far is an act which takes place in what Husserl calls the "natural"[1] or, more generally, the "dogmatic"[2] attitude.

In the "natural attitude," man is directed toward the world and posits it as existing.[3] When he reflects upon himself or perceives others, he considers himself and others as a part of the world.[4] The world which therefore encompasses the totality of being appears with the character of being "in itself." The belief in its existence, even if it is not explicit[5]—and it usually is not[6]—is inherent in any act which has the world as an object. The existence of the world is "the general thesis of the natural attitude."[7]

This attitude is, according to Husserl, *essentially* naïve.[8] The naïveté in question is not the result of some imperfection of the empirical nature of man; it is essentially inherent to all thought directed at objects.[9]

1. *Ideen,* § 27, p. 48.
2. *Ibid.,* § 62, p. 119.
3. *Ibid.,* § 1, p. 7; § 27, p. 48; § 30, pp. 52–53; § 39, p. 71; § 50, p. 94.
4. *Ibid.,* § 27, p. 50; § 29, p. 52; § 33, p. 58.
5. *Ibid.,* § 27, p. 49.
6. *Ibid.,* § 31, p. 53.
7. *Ibid.,* § 30, pp. 52–53; *Phil. als str. Wiss.,* p. 298 [p. 85].
8. On the distinction between naïve, dogmatic, and philosophical sciences, see *Ideen,* § 26, pp. 46–47.
9. *Phil. als str. Wiss.,* p. 299 [p. 87]; *Ideen,* § 62, p. 118; § 79, pp. 156–57.

This naïveté consists in accepting objects as given and existing, without questioning the meaning of this existence and of the "fact of its being given" (*Gegebenheit*). Of course, the "regional ontologies" which we have discussed in the preceding chapter study the essential structure and conditions of the possibility of being, but they ignore one of its dimensions: "what it means that objectivity is." ("Was das besage, dass Gegenständlichkeit sei.")[10] They posit their objects, the essences, as existing.[11] They direct themselves toward essences but ignore the question of the relation of these objects to consciousness and of their place and function in life.[12] This is why, although we are not in the natural attitude in the precise sense of the term when we build ontologies, we are still in the *dogmatic attitude,* which is a more general notion.[13] Aside from the questions that concern the essence and the possibility of existence of objects, one may raise a further question concerning the meaning of their existence, the meaning of the very fact that they are.

Another aspect of the naïveté is that it depends essentially on the ignorance in which one finds oneself, in the natural attitude, concerning the mechanism of life which gives meaning to the objects of the natural attitude, whether these objects are those of perception or of scientific activity. When our sight is directed toward objects we cannot, without shifting it, throw light on the structure of knowledge itself. Therefore we cannot locate these objects in the life [14] which "gives them meaning" and thereby become aware of the genuine intention of life when it is directed toward some object or other; we do not know explicitly "what consciousness is getting at" [15] in each of its acts. The meaning of the object toward which consciousness, because of its intrinsic

10. *Phil. als str. Wiss.,* p. 301 [p. 90].

11. *Ideen,* § 61, p. 117.

12. *Ibid.,* § 94, p. 196n; see also § 134, p. 278; § 147, p. 306; § 150, p. 313.

13. *Ibid.,* § 62, p. 119.

14. *LU,* II, 3 [p. 249].

15. We could not use the last publication of Husserl, "Formale und transzendentale Logik: Versuch einer Kritik der logischen Vernunft," *Jahrbuch für Philosophie und phänomenologische Forschung,* X (1929), because it was published after this work was completed. Yet in reading the general introduction we have seen an agreement between the manner in which Husserl considers the problems of the theory of knowledge and the one we are proposing here.

meaning, *tends*,[16] in some way or other, cannot become visible while we are directly looking at things: the genuine intention of life remains hidden. This is why we may take merely meant objects (in the sense in which meaning is opposed to intuition), with all their inherent ambiguities and obscurities, for objects that are intuitively given.[17] This leads to countless difficulties and contradictions, in which the very meaning of what one knows, and about which one is talking, seems to vanish. This is the origin of the crises and paradoxes in science.

To remedy the naïveté of the natural attitude as we have just described it, we need a theory of knowledge.[18] Instead of living our cognitive life as we do in the naïve attitude, we must take life as our object [19] and ask what is the genuine meaning of the life which is so experienced.[20] What intentions come into play in such and such an experience? What is their structure? How are they related? We must become aware of the genuine intention of life. These are the problems Husserl raises in the *Logische Untersuchungen* in proposing a theory of logical knowledge. He says he is trying to become

> philosophically clear in regard to these same [logical] propositions, that is . . . [he tries to gain] insight into the essence of the modes of cognition which come into play in their utterance . . . together with all such conferments of sense [21] and objective validities as are essentially constituted therein.[22]

From this theory there will follow not only the awareness of the real intention which is present in the thought of logicians but also a reshuffling of logical notions which will consist in looking for them *exclusively* in the intuitive life of consciousness, and in eliminating those that were introduced through the naïveté of the natural attitude.[23]

16. "Formale und transzendentale Logik" uses analogous expressions: "Wissenschaften und Logik . . . haben einen Zwecksinn auf den da beständig hinausgestrebt, hinausgewollt ist" (*ibid.*, p. 8).
17. *LU*, II, 9 [p. 254]; *Ideen*, § 26, p. 47.
18. *LU*, II, 22 [p. 265].
19. *Ibid.*, p. 9 [p. 254].
20. *Ideen*, § 25, p. 45; § 26, p. 47.
21. Acts giving meaning, *Sinngebungen*.
22. *LU*, II, 2 [pp. 248–49]; see also the bottom of p. 6 [252].
23. *Ibid.*, pp. 6, 16–17 [pp. 252, 260].

We can absolutely not rest content with "mere words," i.e. with a merely symbolic understanding of words. . . . Meanings inspired only by remote, confused, inauthentic intuitions—if by any intuitions at all—are not enough. We must go back to the "things themselves." [24]

However, we must also raise more clearly the matter of the place and function of the theory of knowledge in Husserl's philosophy, and we must try to understand what is original in his attitude. We may discover that in the guise of epistemology Husserl pursues interests that are essentially ontological. However, we will save these conclusions for later: the *Logische Untersuchungen* and the *Ideen* explicitly present a theory of knowledge and, if only as an unconscious tribute to the prevalent attitude of the time, Husserl turns this into a central preoccupation.[25]

The problem of knowledge is presented at the beginning of Volume II of the *Logische Untersuchungen* [26] in the following form, which seems indistinguishable from its traditional position: "How are we to understand the fact that the intrinsic being of objectivity becomes 'presented,' 'apprehended' in knowledge, and so ends up by becoming subjective?" [27] According to another passage,[28] Husserl sees the origin of all the difficulties in the theory of knowledge in the "transcendence with respect to knowledge itself" to which the objects of knowledge pretend. Should we then understand that this problem is the one that has so disturbed Lotze [29] and Herbart, the problem of the objective value of subjective representations? Is it just a question of understanding how the laws of thought and the real course of things manifest a rigorous correspondence?

As early as Volume I of the *Logische Untersuchungen*, Husserl asserts the fictitious character of the "apparently profound problem, of the harmony of the subjective course of logical thinking with the real course of external actuality." [30] This remark seems natural to us. If consciousness is essentially intentionality

24. *Ibid.*, p. 6 [p. 252].
25. *Ibid.*, p. 8 [p. 254]; *Ideen*, § 26, p. 47; § 62, p. 118.
26. *LU*, II, 8 [p. 254].
27. See also *Phil. als str. Wiss.*, p. 317 [p. 114].
28. *Ideen*, § 26, p. 47.
29. See Hermann Lotze, *Logik: Drei Bücher vom Denken, vom Untersuchen und vom Erkennen* (Leipsig: S. Hirzel, 1874), pp. 536 f.
30. *LU*, I, 219 [p. 218[.

and "presence in front of being," rather than a reflection of being, how can we speak of a correspondence between the course of thought and the course of things? The problem of Lotze and Herbart presupposes that subjectivity is a closed world, limited to its own representations, which are mere images or symbols of being. Under these conditions the logic which governs thought could only be an "ethics of thought," the laws of thought that we must obey in order for our representations to correspond to being. Then it is natural to wonder how this thought, governed by its own laws, can correspond to an external reality. Husserl himself indicates the close relation which exists between this false problem and the conception of logic as an ethics of thought.[31] However, according to the Husserlian conception of consciousness, we are not directed toward representations or toward mental objects in the form of images or symbols that more or less faithfully represent a real object. We are directed at once toward being.[32] Logic governs thought, not as an autonomous legislation, but because it is the very form of being.

This question—"How are we to understand the fact that the intrinsic being of objectivity becomes 'presented' . . . and so ends up by becoming subjective?"—cannot have the sense that we may be tempted to attribute to it if we conform to our ordinary habits of thought. The idea of a subject which would have to reach and imitate its object is absurd on the face of it.

The question—"How does thought transcend itself?"—expresses only a pseudoproblem. But does it follow that the transcendence of thought is perfectly clear?[33] The intentionality of consciousness is not an "empty look," a transparent light directed toward objects. The transcendence of objects with respect to consciousness is constituted by a rich and "multicolored" set of "intentions." According to what we have said concerning the naïveté of the natural attitude, to clarify the sense of this transcendence is to understand these "intentions" of thought and disentangle the manner, *specific and original for each of them, of constituting a transcendent object.* To understand transcendence is to analyze the intentions of the acts which constitute it. It is to see what consciousness aims at when it transcends itself. We must understand "the mode of being of the *noema,* the man-

31. *Ibid.*
32. *Ideen,* § 43, pp. 78–80.
33. *Ibid.,* § 27, p. 48; § 87, p. 180; § 96, p. 200; § 102, p. 213.

ner in which it must 'lie there' [*wie es liege*] and be 'conscious' in experience." [34] The intrinsic meanings of consciousness must be studied systematically. This study, the study of constitutional problems, is possible. This possibility means that "regular sequences of phenomena,[35] necessarily belonging to the unity of an object which appears, can be perceived intuitively and grasped theoretically." [36]

Therefore the various problems of knowledge are reduced to the problem of how objects are constituted by consciousness. The aim is to find how the sensible (hyletic) data are animated by intentions, how these intentions become united to constitute an object which is one and identical, and how acts become characterized and related when the object constituted by them is given as existing, when the pretension of consciousness to reach its object is justified.[37] Conversely, we must determine which acts give the object as a mere appearance.[38] In the case of spatial things, for example, how does a sequence of acts perceiving an identical thing under ever new aspects successively increase the degree of confirmation and the strength of rational motives? [39] How, on the other hand, can these acts contradict each other so that what was previously acquired becomes transformed into illusion or hallucination? What are the modifications of sense which occur as a result of the "cancellations" (*Durchstreichungen*) that these disappointments [40] impose on the course of experience, etc.? [41] The solution of such problems will also give sense to the notions of "reason," "appearance," "existence," and other fundamental notions of the theory of knowledge. The analysis of intentionality will help us discover the intrinsic meaning of knowledge when it includes the thought of existence, appearance, truth, etc.[42] The descriptions of intuitive acts which we have given in chapter 5 are precisely sketches of phenomeno-

---

34. *Ibid.*, § 96, p. 200.
35. These are internal phenomena.
36. *Ideen*, § 150, p. 315; see also § 135, p. 280; § 142, p. 296.
37. *Ibid.*, § 129, p. 268; § 135, p. 281.
38. *Ibid.*, § 86, pp. 176–77; § 145, pp. 301–2.
39. *Ibid.*, § 138, p. 288.
40. See above, p. 74.
41. *Ideen*, § 138, p. 287; § 151, pp. 317–18; *Phil. als str. Wiss.*, pp. 299–300 [pp. 87–88].
42. *LU*, II, 8–9, 15–16 [pp. 254, 259]. See our article, "Sur les *Ideen* de M. E. Husserl," *Revue philosophique*, CVII (April, 1929), 253, 258.

logical analyses of reason; they try to determine the immanent structure of consciousness in those privileged cases where consciousness not only aims at its object but posits it as existing. In phenomenology, the problem of reason and reality cannot be raised in any other way. It amounts to the following question, which was implied in our posing the problem in chapter 5: "When . . . is the identity of the X [object-pole] which is thought in a *noema* a 'real identity,' and not a 'merely thought identity'; and what does it mean to be 'merely thought'?" [43] The problem must be solved by a noetico-noematic description of the corresponding modes of consciousness. We have dealt with this question in a general way. But the problem of reason, or of "conclusive experience," must be studied in all its forms, which differ in the case of different objects. The idea of "conclusive experience" must be analyzed in all its stages and all its complex structures. [44]

The constitution is different in each region. We have shown that the intuition of sensible objects is different from categorial and eidetic intuition. But in the sphere of individual objects, intuition is not uniform either. The *Einfühlung*, which is an act which reveals the conscious life of others, is a type of intuition different from sensible perception. The experience which reveals animal reality to us is different from that which makes us know, for example, a social phenomenon. Each region of objects has a special "regional ontology" as well as a special mode of being an object of consciousness, i.e., each has a special constitution. [45] Each regional Idea is a "lead" for the discovery of specific modes of constitution in consciousness. [46] "An object which is determined by a regional genus has, inasmuch as it is real, its a priori determined modes of being perceived in general, of being represented, thought, or justified." [47] Even though rigorously determined, [48] constitution differs not only according to regions of objects but also according to the constitutive elements of the region. "The Idea of a region determines entirely a definite series of phenomena. . . . These phenomena depend essentially . . .

---

43. *Ideen*, § 135, p. 281; see also § 153, p. 321; and *passim*.
44. *Ibid.*, § 138, p. 288; § 152, pp. 318–19; § 153, p. 322.
45. *Ibid.*, § 152, p. 318.
46. *Ibid.*, §§ 149, 150, pp. 309–16; § 153, pp. 322–23.
47. *Ibid.*, § 149, p. 309; see also § 79, p. 157; § 138, p. 288; § 142, pp. 296–97.
48. *Ibid.*, § 149, p. 309; see also § 79, p. 157; § 138, p. 288; § 142, pp. 296–97.

on the partial Ideas . . . which compose the regional Idea." [49]
In the case of material things, for example, space, which is a
constitutive element of this region, has a strictly determined
manner of appearing.

> It appears that . . . a reality such as spatial reality can be per-
> ceived only through phenomena in which it is given and must
> necessarily be given in perspectives and orientations which have
> various but always determinate ways of changing. This is true not
> only for us men but also for God, the ideal symbol of absolute
> knowledge.[50]

The Ideas of materiality and temporality serve as guides in
establishing the corresponding modes of consciousness.[51] These
"constitutional problems" are the goal of all the phenomenological
investigations, which themselves serve only as preparation to
the phenomenology of consciousness which studies consciousness with respect to its constitutive function.[52]

However, if "constitutional" problems arise for each region
of objects, in Husserl's philosophy the region of material things
has a privileged place. This region is the foundation of all the
others.[53] This expresses once again what we call Husserl's intellectualism: the primary and fundamental attitude when facing
reality is a pure, disinterested contemplation which considers
things as "merely things." Value predicates or the characters that
make a thing useful *qua* making it useful come only later. The
world of theory comes first.

Since the theory of knowledge is reduced to constitutional
problems, a reversal occurs in the usual manner of bringing up
the question. The problem is no longer to explain the possibility
of the relation of consciousness to its objects. One need only
clarify the meaning of this relation. Notions such as "objectivity,"
"transcendence," "being," etc., that were previously presupposed
but unclarified become in Husserl's theory of knowledge the
principal objects of investigation.[54]

---

49. *Ibid.*, § 150, pp. 314–15.
50. *Ibid.*, § 150, p. 315; see also § 41, pp. 74–75; § 44, pp. 80 f.;
§ 47, p. 90.
51. *Ibid.*, § 150, p. 316.
52. *Ibid.*, § 86, pp. 178–79.
53. *Ibid.*, § 152, p. 319; see also § 119, p. 247.
54. *LU*, II, 21 [p. 265]; *Ideen*, § 86, p. 176; § 135, pp. 280 f.;
§ 147, p. 306; *Phil. als str. Wiss.*, p. 301 [p. 90].

This reversal was made possible only by the discovery of intentionality, which is the essence of consciousness and the true foundation of truth.

Again, the idea of intentionality allows us to constitute, with the help of reflection, the theory of knowledge itself. If, under the notion of consciousness, reflection were to find purely internal elements, it would be incapable of making us understand the "relation of consciousness to its objects." In a consciousness without intentionality reflection would find nothing that belongs to objects, since reflection as such turns away from objects. If, on the contrary, we take intentionality into account, then it itself becomes an object of reflection: the "events" of consciousness on which we reflect all have a relation to objects.[55] Even though we are turning away from the world of things, intentionality reveals it again to us, in consciousness, in the form of *noemata*.[56] Perception cannot be considered without its correlate, "what is perceived *qua* perceived"; desire is nothing without a "desired object," etc. Each *cogito* must be taken in connection with its *cogitatum* and cannot be taken any other way.[57]

Husserl calls this study of consciousness through reflection *phenomenology*.[58] It is a purely descriptive study of consciousness that attempts not to reduce anything and to respect the internal meaning of life and the specific character of all life's modalities.

We may summarize by saying that, for Husserl, the theory of knowledge becomes phenomenolgy and appears as the "self-awareness" (*Selbstbesinnung*) of cognitive life.

> [It] is no more than a thinking over, coming to an evident understanding of, thinking and knowing as such, in their pure generic

55. *Ideen*, § 36, p. 64.
56. *Ibid.*, introduction, p. 1; § 76, p. 142; § 135, pp. 278–79; § 145, pp. 302–3; *Phil. als str. Wiss.*, p. 301 [p. 90].
57. *Ideen*, § 97, p. 202; § 128, p. 265; and especially § 97, pp. 204–5.
58. *Phenomenology* means the science of phenomena. Phenomena are not opposed here to things in themselves, but they are anything which appears to consciousness, anything that can become an object of intuition (*LU*, III, 235 [p. 869]). *Erlebnisse*, as well as the external world, can be objects of intuition and thereby be offered to a phenomenological study in which they will be examined as they appear. In a narrow sense, *phenomenology* means, for Husserl, phenomenology of consciousness. Concerning pure phenomenology, see below, p. 143.

essence, of the specifications and forms that they essentially have, of the immanent structures that their objective relations involve, of the meaning of "validity," "justification," "mediate" and "immediate evidence," and their opposites, as applied to such structures, of the parallel specifications of such Ideas in relation to varying regions of possible objects of knowledge.[59]

Such are the various problems to which phenomenology is applied. Husserl calls this phenomenology "transcendental" because of the specifically transcendental meaning of these problems.[60]

The idea of having a different constitution in each region of objects allows us to draw an interesting consequence for the methodology of science. It would indeed falsify the meaning of objects to conceive all sciences on the same model and to apply the same method to all. This view, which contemporary science has shown to be fortunate, finds here its foundation. (Durkheim's efforts to give sociology its proper object and method seem inspired by the same idea.) The mode of presentation to consciousness of a given category of objects justifies the diversity, with respect not only to their method but also to their problems, of the sciences that apply to different regions. If naturalism has reduced all the spheres of reality to the type of nature, and has thereby falsified its intrinsic meaning, it is because it has neglected this idea.

Constitutional problems have yet another meaning, which has a bearing on more than the theory of knowledge, at least in our opinion. We believe that Husserl himself was very much aware of the consequences of these problems, consequences which emerge in the post-Husserlian philosophy of Heidegger.[61] Husserl's phenomenology goes farther than the goals and problems of a theory of knowledge which would attempt only to clarify the methods and establish the certainty of sciences.

Indeed, what is it that appears to reflection when it is directed toward subjective life in order to learn the constitution of being? When we reflect upon the acts of consciousness, the objects of the natural attitude reappear, in the form of *noemata*, as indispensable correlates of these acts. When considered by reflection, intentional objects are given precisely as they are for the acts

59. *LU*, II, 19 [p. 263].
60. *Ideen*, § 86, p. 178; see also § 97, p. 204.
61. See our Introduction, p. xxxiv.

which think them: a desired object appears "as desired," a willed object "as willed," an imagined object "as imagined"; and these objects appear in their relation to the acts of desire, will, or imagination.[62] These characters of objects that describe their mode of being given to life appear only in a reflection upon life, and they add to the objects a new dimension which escapes the natural attitude.[63] This form of knowledge concerns the very objectivity of objects. In addition to the *quid* of objects that interests the natural attitude, the reflective attitude inquires about the "how," how objects are given, and what it means to be an object.[64] Since being is identical with the various objects of our cognitive as well as our volitive and affective life, the study of the objectivity of objects is reduced to the clarification of the very existence of being.

In consciousness we find being itself in the form of *noemata*. Therefore, we need not ask the following question, which a mere theory of knowledge must ask: how, and by means of what events in cognitive life, do we reach a knowledge of being, and do the objects that we know exist? Our problem is the very meaning of being in each of the special cases in question.

We have spoken of the various modes of objectivity of the objects of different regions. We now see this idea becoming more profound. The objects of different regions have a specific mode of existing. Existence is not an empty term which can be indifferently applied to all species of being, and the essences are not the sole principle of discrimination among objects: we must also consider the mode of existence of objects. Anticipating these conclusions, we tried at the beginning of this work to go back to the very principle of naturalism, which is a certain idea of existence.

The problem of being thus arises with the problems of constitution. To analyze the constitution of an object is to follow the intentions of the life which is directed toward it and the meaning these intentions give to it. Existence is but the mode in which consciousness meets its objects or the role played by objects in

62. *Ideen*, § 88, pp. 182–83; § 95, pp. 198–99.
63. *Ibid.*, § 150, pp. 313–14; § 145, p. 307. When Husserl insists (*ibid.*, § 108, p. 220) on the fact that noematic characters "are not determined by reflection," he can only mean that we grasp them by looking at the noematic side of intentionality and not by attributing to the *noema* characters which are found by reflection in the *noesis*.
64. *Ibid.*, § 76, p. 142; § 88, p. 183; § 93, p. 193; and especially § 97, pp. 204–5; *Phil. als str. Wiss.*, p. 301 [p. 91].

the concrete life of consciousness, since the very origin of being is in life. Hence, *noemata* (i.e., "what is represented *qua* represented," "what is desired *qua* desired"), inseparable.[65] from the *noeses* from which they derive their meaning, make visible the role played in concrete life by such and such a category of objects as it is revealed by the intrinsic meaning of life. Noetico-noematic descriptions of the constitution of objects are the great task of phenomenology, which, far from being a mere theory of knowledge, has an exceptional ontological value. The theory and critique of knowledge are, in fact, but corollaries and applications of this fundamental ontology.

There is another way in which the phenomenology of constitutional problems is more than a theory of knowledge. However, according at least to the letter of his philosophy, Husserl did not explicitly engage himself in that direction.

Indeed, the theory of knowledge, understood as an analysis of cognitive life, does not exhaust all of life.

We have shown at length the privileged place granted by the *Logische Untersuchungen* to theoretical life. We have seen that acts of valuing, willing, etc., in all their forms are based on a representation. This preeminence of theory, established in the *Logische Untersuchungen*, has never been denounced by Husserl. But, in this respect, *Ideen* mark a progress: they assert that non-theoretical acts also constitute objects that have a new and ir-reducible ontological structure. These acts, as well as the acts of judgment and representation, are "objectivizing." We derived this consequence at the beginning of our work when discussing intentionality. There is a detailed presentation in that chapter. If we are now returning to those theses, it is to show how they fecundate phenomenology and carry it beyond the theory of knowledge.

> All acts in general are similarly "objectivizing," whether they are acts of affectivity or of will, and they constitute objects in an original way. They are the necessary sources of different regions of being, and thereby, also, of the corresponding ontologies. For example, an act of valuation constitutes an *axiological* object [*Gegenständlichkeit*], which is distinct from the world of mere things and which belongs to another region of being.[66]

65. *Ideen*, § 93, p. 193.
66. *Ibid.*, § 117, p. 244.

The new characters introduced into being by those acts are not new properties, that is, new predicates which leave objects on the same level of existence. They belong to a completely new "dimension of meaning." [67] They do not constitute

> new determinations of *things that are merely things,* but *values* of things . . . , beauty and ugliness, goodness and meanness; they constitute useful objects, works of art, machines, books, actions [*die Handlung*], deeds [*die Tat*], etc.[68]

It follows that, in addition to theoretical truths, there can be "practical and axiological truths." [69] The Husserlian conception of truth makes this easy to understand. Since truth does not belong essentially to judgments but to intuitive intentionality, our contact with the world of useful and practical values has a legitimate right to be also considered as truth. In this case we are dealing with a specific intuition, which, as we ascertained in chapters 4 and 5, does not seem to be an act of theoretical contemplation. To be in contact with the world of values certainly does not mean to know it theoretically.[70] The existence of a value—its mode of presenting itself to life—does not have the same ontological structure as theoretically represented beings.

Not only the phenomenology of knowledge but that of consciousness in general seeks to clarify these modes of existing by going back to the origin of objects in life and by pursuing the study of their constitution in consciousness.[71]

However, even if the constitution of these objects in life is heterogeneous to the constitution of theoretical objects, theoretical objects must still serve as their basis.[72] In this respect *Ideen* agrees with the assertions of the *Logische Untersuchungen*. We have mentioned the privileged role of the phenomenology of material things that, in essence, expresses the primacy of theory.

But the primacy of theoretical consciousness in the constitution of being is, according to Husserl, deeper yet. Although the

67. *Ibid.,* § 116, p. 239.
68. *Ibid.,* § 116, pp. 239–40; see also § 95, p. 198; § 117, p. 241; § 121, p. 250; and especially § 152, p. 319.
69. *Ibid.,* § 136, p. 290; § 147, pp. 305 f.
70. See *ibid.,* § 37, p. 66.
71. *Ibid.,* § 108, p. 221.
72. *Ibid.,* § 95, pp. 197–98; § 102, pp. 213 f.; § 116, p. 239; § 119, p. 247.

meaning of existence (or of objectivity, to speak a Husserlian language) is different in each category of objects, and although each category is constituted in life in a different manner, a theoretical position which Husserl calls a *doxic thesis* is always included in the act which posits these different objects as existing. "An act of positing posits [*ein positionaler Akt setzt*], but whatever the quality of this position, it is also doxic." [73] This doxic thesis is the element of intentionality which, according to Husserl, thinks of objects as existing. It is because each act of consciousness includes a doxic thesis that the objects of these acts —values, useful objects, or aesthetic objects—exist. Husserl's assertion here demonstrates that the notion of existence remains for him tightly bound to the notion of theory, to the notion of knowledge, despite all the elements in his system which seem to lead us to a richer notion of existence than mere presence of an object to a contemplative consciousness. We have tried to mark out these elements, going sometimes beyond the letter of Husserl's theory. However, for Husserl, it is inasmuch as we know an object theoretically that we have access to it as existing. The role of the doxic theses, included in all the theses of consciousness, obliges us to say that in a certain respect Husserl's phenomenology is not free from the theory of knowledge. It seems to us that this restriction diminishes the scope and the interest of the assertion that all acts of consciousness are "objectivizing acts" and constitute being. Let us also note incidentally the dogmatism involved in juxtaposing, without justification, the theoretical, practical, and affective life, following a classification inherited from traditional anthropology and psychology. In any event, the concrete phenomenological analyses elaborated by Husserl belong almost exclusively to the phenomenology of knowledge.

The general considerations to which we have devoted the preceding pages have shown the considerable philosophical interest, present in the Husserlian attitude, of the study of consciousness and the ontological dignity of the problems raised in it. We have noticed the exceptional role played by reflection, whose highest title is to be philosophical intuition.

Philosophical intuition must now be more directly characterized, still without mentioning the *phenomenological reduction*

73. *Ibid.*, § 117, p. 243; see also § 134, pp. 277 f.; § 117, p. 241; § 121, p. 251.

which, according to Husserl, introduces us into the realm of phenomenology. It is true that philosophical intuition is identical with a reflection on a "phenomenologically reduced" consciousness, but we shall save this point until later in order to be able to understand the meaning of the phenomenological reduction as a function of the whole system.

"The phenomenological method moves exclusively among acts of reflection." [74] *Erlebnisse* are experienced, and their existence consists in the fact of being conscious. Life, however, is not to itself its own object through the mere fact of being lived and conscious. To live and to have life for an object are not the same thing.[75] Yet, by virtue of its very nature, conscious life can not only be lived but can also be taken as an object by consciousness, after undergoing a certain modification which transforms it from a nonreflective into a reflective state.[76] This transformation is possible only through a falling back of consciousness upon itself. This falling back of consciousness upon itself legitimizes, for Husserl, the use of the term *reflection.*[77]

By *reflection*, Husserl means "all the modes of grasping immanent essences and all the modes of immanent experience." [78] It includes, therefore, "the acts in which the flow of life, with all its numerous events (the various moments of *Erlebnisse* and intentions), becomes distinguished with evidence and susceptible of analysis." [79]

This last quotation demonstrates the intuitive character of acts of reflection: their object is given "in person," consciousness is "in person" present to itself. It also shows that there is a multiplicity of modes of internal intuition: perception is not the only reflective intuitive act. In fact, an act of reflection may occur in memory, in imagination, or in the *Einfühlung*.[80] The general theory of intuition therefore applies to reflection. We find there again the parallel of imagination and memory and the exceptional and privileged role of perception. Truth is adequation of thought, as a purely signifying intention, to an object given in

74. *Ibid.,* § 77, p. 144.
75. *Ibid.,* p. 145; § 38, p. 67.
76. *Ibid.,* § 78, p. 148.
77. *Ibid.,* § 150, p. 314.
78. *Ibid.,* § 78, p. 148.
79. *Ibid.,* p. 147.
80. *Ibid.,* § 38, p. 68; § 77, p. 145; § 78, p. 148.

intuition, an intuition which grasps an object which is present in all its concrete reality, "in person."

However, immanent intuition, reflection, has a privileged character with respect to the intuition directed at the external world. It is the character of adequation which, as we have tried to show, is based upon the existence of its object, consciousness, and has allowed us to posit consciousness as absolute. In the *Logische Untersuchungen* [81] Husserl studies intuition in general and distinguishes various degrees of extension, vivacity, and real content. It is evident that external perception, by its very nature, cannot realize these three characters to their highest degree. We have seen that external objects are always given together with a set (a "horizon") of merely meant moments. Perception can have vivacity, but the totality of the intentional object evidently cannot be realized in it.[82] It is only internal intuition which can present the ideal of adequation. Only internal intuition has its object all at once before itself.[83] Even if a certain inadequation is also proper to immanent perception, because of the temporal character of consciousness and the fact that the objects of reflection are constantly falling into the past,[84] for Husserl this inadequation [85] is of another type than that of transcendent perception. As we have shown,[86] there is an abyss between the adequation of internal perception and the inadequation of external perception.[87]

Once reflection has been posited as the act through which consciousness becomes explicitly aware of itself, should we not ask whence reflection derives the right to grasp conscious life as it *is*? The whole philosophical value of reflection consists in allowing us to grasp our life, and the world in our life, such as they are prior to reflection.[88] Hence, if *Erlebnisse* can be revealed to consciousness only after being modified by reflection, then only modified states of consciousness would be accessible to us and not life in its original form. Therefore we must examine the acts of reflection closely. We shall then be able to decide

81. *LU*, III, 83–84 [p. 735]; see above, chap, 5, p. 70.
82. See above, chap. 2, p. 21.
83. *Ideen*, § 144, p. 298.
84. *Ibid.*, § 77, p. 146.
85. *Ibid.*, § 44, pp. 82 f.
86. See above, chap. 2, p. 32.
87. *Ideen*, § 49, p. 93.
88. *Ibid.*, § 79, pp. 153–54.

whether phenomenology can reach life in general or only reflected life.[89]

There are real modifications of life under the influence of reflection. First, the very fact of reflection gives to life the character of "being reflected," and one may wonder "whether, in the end, the *Erlebnisse* that are subjected to it are not transformed thereby into something different *toto coelo*." [90] Furthermore, conscious life has a duration, and reflective acts can grasp perceptively only the present instant, the present surging of life, the *Urimpression*, while other moments drown in the past or emerge in the future. Even the immediate past and future are perceived only by an act of "retention" or "protention," specific acts of reflection to which both memory and perception collaborate.[91] But the certainty of the *cogito*, which we discussed so much in chapter 2, and which is founded in the mode of existence of life, seems to belong only to the perception of the present instant, while it seems possible to doubt the data of retention. Finally, under the action of reflection, phenomena undergo a qualitative modification: reflected-upon joy and anger are of a different type than spontaneous joy and anger.[92]

Husserl responds to all these important objections in terms of a principle to which he gives a formal character: it is absurd to contest the right of reflection to attain conscious life as it really is, because it amounts to presupposing what one denies, it is falling back into the contradiction characteristic of skepticism.[93] Indeed, whoever asserts that he doubts the cognitive capacity of reflection makes at least one assertion about his doubt, but this assertion is the result of reflection.[94] Likewise, when speaking of the modification to which spontaneous life is submitted when it becomes an object of reflection, one presupposes the possibility of knowing life prior to reflection, for otherwise one could not speak of modification. But it is precisely this possibility which is contested by skepticism.[95] Finally, one may not deny the value of

---

89. *Ibid.*, pp. 154–55.
90. *Ibid.*, § 78, p. 151; see also § 78, p. 148; § 98, p. 205; § 77, pp. 146–47.
91. *Ibid.*, § 77, pp. 145–46; § 78, p. 149.
92. *Ibid.*, § 70, p. 130; § 75, p. 141.
93. *Ibid.*, § 79, p. 155; § 20, p. 37; *LU*, I, 110 [p. 340].
94. *Ideen*, § 79, p. 155.
95. *Ibid.*, pp. 155–56.

reflection because, if reflection had no value, one could say nothing about reflection itself.[96]

This formal refutation of skepticism is insufficient, and Husserl seems to recognize this.[97] What is needed is a reflection upon reflection, a sort of critique of phenomenology, a critique of the possibilities and of the rights of reflection.[98] We must examine more closely how far the certainty of reflection goes, how through modifications it can grasp a primitive state. (Despite its modifications, we still distinguish in an object of reflection the fact that it has existed independently of reflection.[99] What is grasped in perceptual reflection is characterized, in principle, as something which not only is and endures during the act of reflection but which was already there previously.)[100] In *Ideen*, Husserl gives only the result of his analyses. According to him, the absolute right of perceptual reflection extends not only to the present instant but also to the sphere of immediate protentions and retentions, to what is *still* experienced and to what is *on the point* of being experienced.[101] Our life is not limited to the present instant; its horizon encompasses past and future. The critique of reflection must therefore establish, in addition to the right of reflective perception, the right of memory to grasp the past. This right does not wholly and essentially apply to our past: we may be mistaken about it. "It is purely relative and can be superseded without losing its character of right." [102] However, we can be certain of the mere existence of our past by virtue of the very structure of time. Consciousness, inasmuch as it exists and endures, can have neither beginning nor end.[103] Each instant of time requires a past in which to disappear and a future from which to emerge.[104]

96. *Ibid.*, p. 156.
97. *LU*, II, 10 [p. 255]; *Ideen*, § 66, p. 124.
98. *Ideen*, § 77, p. 147; § 79, p. 156. This study of reflection through reflection is not a vicious circle. It is only the return on the self common to all the sciences of principles, such as logic. There is a vicious circle only when the conclusion is involved in the premises. Such is not the relation here; the reflection which must derive the rights of reflection will be justified by its own results. See *Ideen*, § 65, p. 122; *LU*, I, § 19, pp. 53 ff. [pp. 92 ff.].
99. *Ideen*, § 77, p. 145.
100. *Ibid.*, § 45, p. 83.
101. *Ibid.*, § 78, pp. 150–51.
102. *Ibid.*, p. 151; § 140, p. 293.
103. *Ibid.*, §§ 81, 82, pp. 163–65.
104. *Ibid.*, § 82, pp. 164–65; *Phil. als str. Wiss.*, p. 313 [p. 107].

Thus as we examine the results of the critique of reflection, we see that the reservations raised above were exaggerated, even though it is necessary to set limits to the pretentions of reflection. These limits have, according to Husserl, their foundation in the existence of consciousness, and it would be absurd to treat them as imperfections.[105]

To study the constitution of objects in life, we may use intuitive reflection and use it at all the levels of conscious life. It can describe the structure of a *noema*[106] which is inseparable from a *noesis*, and it may also study all the articulations of all the levels of more complex noetico-noematic structures. For example, such are the *noemata* which Husserl calls *reiterated* (*iteriert*).[107] These are *noemata* which are themselves object-cores:[108] I may remember a memory of a perception.[109] An intuitive look may travel through the various levels of articulation of a *noema* (this is an inherent possibility)[110] and may stop at any one of them. It is also necessary that intuitive looks be limited to the complexity of what is given and respect its intrinsic meaning without introducing anything indirectly—as through reasoning, for example.[111]

Reflection need not be limited to *noeses* and *noemata*. *Hyletic* elements also participate in the constitution of objects. A reflection upon hyletic data—upon sensations, for example— follows this constitution down to the hyletic level, describes the manner in which the hyletic level is animated by intentions (apprehensions),[112] and describes the temporal structure of consciousness.[113] In short, phenomenological reflection is an intuitive look directed at life in all the fullness of life's concrete forms. It is an attempt to understand life and, on that basis, to understand the world, life's intentional object.

If philosophical intuition were only a reflection upon life, philosophy would be reduced to an empirical science occupied with the factual states of life and disdainful of all a priori law.

105. *Ideen*, § 79, p. 157.
106. *Ibid.*, § 98, p. 206.
107. *Ibid.*, § 100, p. 211.
108. See above, chap. 4, pp. 54–55.
109. *Ideen*, § 100, pp. 210–11.
110. *Ibid.*, § 101, p. 212.
111. *Ibid.*, § 89, pp. 183–84; *LU*, II, 11 [p. 256]; *Ideen*, § 108, p. 221.
112. *Ideen*, § 97, p. 203; § 86, p. 176.
113. *Ibid.*, § 81, p. 163.

Outside the realm of contingency one would find only the instantaneous *cogito* which is necessary despite being factual. Furthermore, we have emphasized that the empirical sciences are possible only when the corresponding ontologies are established. But if we are dealing with the science of the facts of consciousness, where is the a priori science that can serve as its basis? [114]

In reflection upon consciousness, as in the direct intuition of the world, ideation is possible. "Each *Erlebnis* in the flow considered by a reflective act has its own individual essence that can be grasped intuitively; it has a content that can be considered in itself with its own character." [115] *Erlebnisse* have essences, a necessary structure, and as such they are governed by eidetic laws. Consciousness is an individual *concrete* object,[116] and the set of highest genera that constitute it forms a region. Consciousness is a region and the source of an ontology. Constitutional problems will be solved by means of the eidetic intuition of consciousness. The structure of the act which constitutes each category of objects is a necessary structure and has its foundation in the eidetic laws of these acts. All the descriptions of conscious life which we have given so far concerning the structure of time, intentionality, the correlation between *noema* and *noesis*, reflection and the possibility of reflection—all these are a priori and given in the eidetic intuition of reflection.

Phenomenology is an eidetic, descriptive science of consciousness.[117] Of course, one may wonder whether conscious life in all the multiplicity of its qualitatively distinct forms can be fully covered by essences. The Bergsonian antinomy between intellect and conscious life may have some validity. How can the duration of conscious life, whose originality is in no way contested by Husserl,[118] be grasped in the rigid frameworks of the intellect? What we have said above of the possibility of inexact essences may help us to understand how the intellect can cover the field of conscious life without making it "spatial." [119] Besides abstract

114. *Ibid.*, § 62, p. 119; § 60, p. 113.
115. *Ibid.*, § 34, p. 61; *Phil. als str. Wiss.*, p. 314 [p. 110].
116. In the sense indicated above, see chap. 6, pp. 111–112.
117. *Ideen*, § 75, p. 139.
118. On the continuity between consciousness and duration, see *Ideen*, § 75, pp. 139 f.; § 81, pp. 162, 164; *Phil. als str. Wiss.*, p. 313 [p. 107].
119. See above, chap. 6; see also *Ideen*, § 75, p. 139.

rationality and concrete intuition, Husserl indicates a third alternative.

Phenomenological reflection is ideative reflection. It uses the
concrete perceived state of consciousness toward which it is
directed as an example in order to return to its essence. But perception is not required for ideation. To use as "example" an object of imagination is enough and even better.[120]

> It belongs to the general essence of the immediate apprehension
> of essences . . . to take place on the basis of *a mere re-presenta-*
> *tion [Vergegenwärtigung]* of exemplary singularities.[121]

This gives the phenomenologist the freedom necessary to detach
himself from what is actually given and survey the sphere of all
possibilities. He thereby enters into the domain of essences
whose meaning is to imply an infinity of possible "examples." [122]
It appears once more that eidetic truths are a priori and that,
despite the fact that they are necessarily given by means of
examples, they concern essential possibilities. They are totally
independent of actual perceptions.[123] Husserl says, paradoxically,
"Fiction is the vital element of phenomenology as well as all
other eidetic sciences." [124]

The clarity manifested by the intuition of essences, especially
when they are not too general,[125] depends on the clarity of the
intuition of the individual on whom the intuition of essences is
based.[126] This clarity is not necessarily that of perception; it may
also be that of imagination; but it must never be lacking. Here is
one of the most laborious tasks of phenomenology. It is not easy
to practice the intuition of essences, and many times Husserl
insists on these difficulties.[127] He recommends a long apprentice-
ship for beginners; he advises them to practice with perception
before using imagination. The study of conscious life as it appears in history, in works of art, and in poetry is also useful.

But *the long effort required by phenomenology in order to*

120. *Ideen*, § 4, pp. 12, 13; § 70, p. 130.
121. *Ibid.*, § 70, p. 129; see also § 79, p. 153.
122. *Ibid.*, § 70, p. 131.
123. *Ibid.*, § 34, p. 60.
124. *Ibid.*, § 70, p. 132.
125. *Ibid.*, § 69, p. 129.
126. *Ibid.*, § 67, p. 125.
127. *Ibid.*, § 71, p. 132; § 61, p. 117; *LU*, II, 11 [p. 256].

reach intuition does not have the metaphysical meaning that Bergson, for example, attributes to the efforts of intuition, which, in his terms, has, to say the least, very narrow ties with acts of freedom. We shall return to this in our conclusion. The efforts necessary to learn how to intuit essences, as well as the other even greater efforts which Husserl relates to the *phenomenological reduction* (about which we have yet to speak), are never, at least in Husserl's presently published writings, studied in their relation to the nature of consciousness.[128] Philosophical intuition is not, as in Bergson's philosophy or in the "philosophies of life," an act in which all the vital forces are engaged, an act which plays an important role in the destiny of life. For Husserl, philosophical intuition is a reflection on life considered in all its concrete fullness and wealth, a life which is considered but no longer lived. The reflection upon life is divorced from life itself, and one cannot see its ties with the destiny and the metaphysical essence of man. The natural attitude is not purely contemplative; the world is not purely an object of scientific investigation. Yet it seems that man *suddenly* accomplishes the phenomenological reduction by a purely theoretical act of reflection on life. Husserl offers no explanation for this change of attitude and does not even consider it a problem. Husserl does not raise the metaphysical problem of the situation of the *Homo philosophus*.

The characterization of philosophical intuition could not be complete without a study of the phenomenological reduction.

How does the study of consciousness, as we have analyzed it, differ from psychology? This is a natural question to ask. If we take phenomenology as the foundation and starting point of philosophy, does this not amount to identifying philosophy and psychology? [129] Are we not falling back into the psychologism against which Husserl fought so hard in the *Logische Untersuchungen*?

We have already noted that the critique of psychologism in Volume I of the *Logische Untersuchungen* is directed only toward bad psychology (naturalistic psychology) and makes room for a good, phenomenological psychology. But, according to Husserl, even after psychology is purified from all psychologistic and naturalistic admixtures, even after intentionality is recognized

128. Concerning the efforts necessary in order to enter the realm of phenomenology, see *Ideen*, introduction, pp. 2–3; § 9, p. 20; § 87, p. 180; and *passim*. Husserl only asserts them.

129. *Ibid.*, introduction, p. 2.

as the essential structure of consciousness, we have still not reached phenomenology as philosophy, *pure phenomenology.*[130]

It is characteristic of the psychologistic attitude that it is a science of the world. The totality of reality which we call the world also includes man, his body, and his psychological states. Man is a part of the world, as well as mountains and trees are.[131] Hence the various psychological disciplines study man only as a natural being, having a body,[132] and dependent on the world and on world causality. Being tied to the world, consciousness in some way participates in the existence of the world.

> The absolute in itself [consciousness] can lose its immanence and acquire a character of transcendence. We immediately see that it can do so only by participating in some way in transcendence in the original sense of the term, i.e., the transcendence of material nature.[133]

If the existence of the world is not absolutely certain and if, as we saw in chapter 2 above, it contains within itself a possibility of nonbeing, then man and consciousness, as studied by psychology, must and do present the same character. "The empirical ego is as much a case of transcendence [134] as the physical thing." [135]

However, reflection upon consciousness reveals with evidence, in the *cogito*, an absolute existence that must be admitted as such. "But," says Husserl, "if there is really such an adequate self-evidence—who indeed could deny it?—how can we avoid assuming a pure ego?" [136] We must conclude that the absolute consciousness of the *cogito*, the only type of consciousness which has been considered in our analyses so far, is not identical with psychological consciousness. Husserl calls the absolute consciousness pure or transcendental consciousness. The true fountain of being, the realm of its constitution, is therefore not psychological consciousness.[137] Empirical consciousness as studied by psy-

130. *LU*, III, 235–36 [p. 862].
131. *Ideen*, introduction, pp. 3–4; § 33, p. 58; § 39, pp. 69, 70; *Phil. als str. Wiss.*, pp. 298–99 [p. 86].
132. *Ideen*, § 53, p. 103; § 76, p. 143.
133. *Ibid.*, § 53, p. 103.
134. "Transcendent object" is opposed here to the notion of "immanent object," which is pure consciousness in the specific mode of its existence and to which transcendent objects are totally foreign.
135. *LU*, II, 357 [p. 544n]; *Ideen*, § 39, p. 70.
136. *LU*, II, 357n [p. 544n]. The "pure ego" is opposed here to the "empirical ego" of psychologists. See *Ideen*, § 54, p. 106.
137. *Ideen*, § 51, p. 95.

chologists does not capture in any way the originality and first surging of our life.[138] The original surging of life is given in the evidence of the *cogito*. Even when they speak of intentionality, psychologists treat consciousness as causally related to nature through the body.[139] "Naïve man" also treats consciousness as a thing among things. This means that consciousness is not grasped in its purity but is interpreted—or, following Husserl's expression, "perceived"—in relation to the world. "It is according to a particular mode of apprehension or experience, a particular mode of *apperception*, that consciousness is, so to speak, *put in touch* [with the world] and *realized*." [140] Absolute consciousness, perceived as psychological consciousness, of course loses nothing of its nature; its mode of appearing does not change, and yet it is not the same consciousness. "It remains in itself what it is: absolute being. But it is not perceived as such . . . , it is perceived as a thing and this specific apperception constitutes a *sui generis* transcendence." [141] "Hence, . . . a natural, psychophysical individual is constituted [in the eyes of absolute consciousness] a man or an animal as a unit based on a body." [142]

In summary, we must distinguish between psychological and phenomenological consciousness. It is the latter which is genuinely first and concrete; the former is constituted for the latter as any other transcendent object. The mode in which consciousness is constituted in pure or transcendental [143] consciousness can and must be an object of study. Thus we can clarify the meaning of that "apperception" in which the philosophical problem of the relation between mind and body seems to lie.

There is another great difference between the phenomenological attitude and the psychological attitude. In the psychological attitude, although we are directed toward life, we are oriented toward the world, which we posit as existing and as including life, the object of our investigations. Of course, in the psychological reflection we find the hyletico-noetico-noematic structure of consciousness, but in the psychological attitude the world of

138. *Ibid.*, § 53, p. 104.
139. *Ibid.*, p. 103.
140. *Ibid. Realization* here means the act of imposing the ontological structure of a *res*, of a thing; it is a *reification*.
141. *Ibid.*, p. 104.
142. *Ibid.*
143. This is what Husserl calls the phenomenological consciousness. See *ibid.*, § 33, p. 59.

noemata does not represent the real world recovered at the source and in the modes of its constitution. (This does happen, however, in the phenomenological attitude.) One may study *noemata* without giving up the natural attitude and, consequently, without clarifying the existence of the world. The existence of the world does not require that we suspend the act of positing the world in order to clarify this act itself. In the psychological attitude,[144] the belief in the existence of the world remains and, even when it is not explicit, it is inherent to the study of consciousness. In a word, as it turns itself toward life and its intrinsic meaning, psychology cannot recognize that it is going back to the source of being but believes that it is studying only one of its regions.

The distinctions which we have just made between psychology and phenomenology are not a condemnation of the former [145] but only describe its scope and limits: psychology is not philosophy.[146] The world exists for a psychologist as it does for any other scientist. Psychology is a science of the world with rights that must be delineated by phenomenology,[147] rights that are as genuine as those of physics or chemistry. Moreover, the ties between (phenomenological) psychology and phenomenology are so narrow [148] that the propositions established by psychology may coincide word for word with the results of the phenomenology of consciousness.[149] Both phenomenology and psychology study one and the same consciousness.[150] However, the meaning of the two sciences is different: one is philosophy and studies pure consciousness, the other is psychology and studies a "naturalized" consciousness.[151]

---

144. In this whole passage, we are discussing phenomenological psychology, which is limited to the study of the intrinsic meaning of immanence but admits of a passage to psychophysics and to psychophysiology. This is phenomenology in general, as opposed to pure phenomenology. *LU*, III, 235 [p. 862]; *Phil, als str. Wiss.*, p. 314 [p. 109].

145. *Ideen*, introduction, p. 2.

146. *Phil. als str. Wiss.*, p. 302 [pp. 91–92].

147. *Ibid.*, p. 304 [p. 94].

148. *Ibid.*, p. 302 [p. 92]; *Ideen*, § 30, p. 52; § 53, pp. 104 f.; § 79, pp. 158 f.

149. *Ideen*, § 76, pp. 143–44; § 53, pp. 104 f.; *Phil. als str. Wiss.*, p. 321 [p. 120].

150. *Ideen*, § 33, p. 58; § 76, p. 143.

151. *Ibid.*, § 53, p. 104; *Phil. als str. Wiss.*, p. 302 [p. 92].

Psychology, which places consciousness in nature, will never be able to understand its specific existence. Psychology will never be able to understand that to be an ego in the world is not to be in the world like a thing. The character of *In-esse* is quite different in both cases. Hence the great merit of the theory of the phenomenological reduction (the method which leads us to the phenomenological consciousness) is to have shown, at least negatively, that the existence of consciousness and its relation to the world must be conceived in a way totally different from the existence of a part in a whole.

Empiricism has identified transcendental and psychological consciousness; that is its great mistake. The origin of this error can be found in Descartes. In Locke, Berkeley, and Hume it reaches a manifest absurdity, as a purely naturalistic study of consciousness leads to the negation of the reality and categories of nature.

However, the distinction between psychological and phenomenological consciousness, as conceived by Husserl, is directed as strongly toward someone like Fichte, who identifies transcendental consciousness with a pure-ego transcendent with respect to the concrete consciousness that we are.[152] Transcendental consciousness is not any farther from us than psychological consciousness; it is closer, since it is the genuine consciousness, in opposition to consciousness "as a thing." Psychological consciousness itself is constituted in transcendental consciousness.[153]

The phenomenological reduction is precisely the method by which we are going back to concrete man. Because of it, we discover the field of pure consciousness where we can practice philosophical intuition.[154] The characters of transcendental consciousness allow us to understand the meaning of this operation.

Instead of positing the existence of the world as we do in the natural attitude, we are suspending our judgment, as Descartes does when he exercises his doubt with respect to all his assertions. But our doubt has a different meaning from the

152. Husserl says: "Andererseits ist die Welt der transzendenten res durchaus auf Bewusstsein, und *zwar nicht auf logisch erdachtes, sondern actuelles angewiesen*" (*Ideen*, § 49, p. 92; my italics).

153. *Ibid.*, § 54, p. 105; § 76, p. 143.

154. *Ibid.*, introduction, p. 3; § 32, p. 56; § 33, pp. 58 f.; § 50, pp. 94 f.; § 56, p. 108; and *passim*.

Cartesian doubt: it is purely ephectic.[155] Descartes's suspension of judgment has, according to Husserl, the character of a universal negation.[156] But we posit neither the existence nor the non-existence of the world.[157] We "disconnect," we "bracket," the position of its existence.[158] We do not assert existence, and we do not deny it. We want to remain neutral with respect to this assertion and study it.[159] Husserl writes: "it [the thesis which posits the world as existing] *remains there* as what has been bracketed." [160]

However, as we suspend the judgments made in the natural attitude, we still face the consciousness which makes these judgments and resists the epochē [161] of the phenomenological reduction.[162] We cannot "exclude" or "disconnect" the judgments that apply to consciousness. The absolute and specific existence of consciousness, which we have clarified at length, guards it against such exclusion. By virtue of this existence, the act which posits consciousness has an absolute certainty, the certainty of the *cogito*.

Thus, the phenomenological epochē leads us to considering conscious life. Conscious life is revealed as an intention directed at being and asserting the existence of its objects. These can be found in consciousness in the form of *noemata,* which are inseparable from consciousness.[163] They are found "in brackets," to use Husserl's expression, or "reduced" to what they are for consciousness and ready to be studied by phenomenology.

The phenomenological epochē does not destroy the truths proper to the natural attitude but wants only to clarify their sense.[164] "With respect to each thesis we can . . . practice a specific epochē, a certain suspension of judgment which agrees

---

155. We must insist that the reduction is different from Cartesian doubt. Cartesian doubt is considered here only to emphasize certain characters of the reduction.

156. *Ideen,* § 31, p. 55.

157. *Ibid.,* p. 54.

158. *Ibid.*

159. *Ibid.,* § 90, p. 187.

160. *Ibid.,* § 31, p. 54.

161. This term is introduced in *ibid.,* § 31, p. 56.

162. *Ibid.,* § 33, p. 59.

163. *Ibid.,* § 76, p. 142; § 135, pp. 278–79; § 145, pp. 302–3; and *passim.*

164. *Ibid.,* § 90, p. 187.

with the unshaken and unshakable conviction provided by the evidence of truth." [165]

The consciousness to which the epochē leads us is transcendental and not psychological. Psychological consciousness cannot be posited as absolute or, consequently, resist the reduction, since it is itself, like the rest of the world, subject to the epochē. There is another reason why our attitude should not be confused with that of a psychologist reflecting upon consciousness. A psychologist posits the existence of the world at the same time as he reflects on the act which posits this existence. But the phenomenological epochē forbids us to proceed in that way. We do not identify ourselves with the life in which objects are posited. We become in some way detached from ourselves and limit ourselves to the consideration of life. We give no credence, in other words, to the thesis we are considering. [166]

To summarize: because of the epochē we reach consciousness since it alone subsists as the sole object of our judgments once every proposition about the world has become forbidden to us. But also, and for the same reason, it is not a psychological but a transcendental consciousness which is revealed to us in the phenomenological reduction.

By forbidding the use of any assertion that includes the thesis of the existence of the world, we also eliminate the use, as a premise, of any judgment made in the natural attitude. Consequently, we do not presuppose science, [167] either of nature or of the mind, either experimental or eidetic (regional ontology). [168] We do not presuppose ourselves *qua* "persons" living in the world; we presuppose neither other persons nor God. [169] We free phenomenology from all foreign presuppositions, as is becoming to a philosophical science, "a science of first principles," [170] which proceeds only through immediate intuitions. [171] In the sphere of consciousness we still find, in the form of *noemata,* all the propositions of science with their particular mode of being con-

165. *Ibid.,* § 31, p. 55.
166. *Ibid.,* § 90, p. 187.
167. *Ibid.,* § 32, pp. 56–57.
168. *Ibid.,* §§ 58–60, pp. 111–15.
169. *Ibid.,* § 58, p. 110.
170. *Ibid.,* § 56, p. 108; see also § 59, p. 113; § 60, p. 115; § 63, p. 121.
171. *Ibid.,* § 59, p. 113.

stituted for consciousness; [172] this is the aspect in which they interest us. We find them because to consider consciousness is to consider it in its relation with the world, with objects, and with *Sachverhalte*. We do not discuss the value and scope of the judgments and propositions of science, since they do not serve as premises to phenomenological research; [173] but we do ask how they are constituted, i.e., what they mean for life. Phenomenology has no other goal than to place again the world of objects—objects of perception, science, or logic—in the concrete web of our life and to understand them on that basis.[174] This is exactly what noetico-noematic analyses mean.

The body itself, whose relation to consciousness forms what is called in psychology the mind-body problem, does not disappear in the reduction. It is first constituted by a set of *Erlebnisse* and internal sensations. It is also given as an object having a specific structure and playing a privileged role in the totality of experience. As to the relation between consciousness and the body, understood as a natural object, only a phenomenological analysis of psychological apperception can clarify its meaning. The problem seems to us to be reduced to knowing what this relation means, i.e., how it is constituted in transcendental life.

Is the reduction a temporary attitude like the Cartesian doubt? We believe that, by showing the place of the reduction among the problems and goals of phenomenology, we have shown that it is not. Far from being temporary, the reduction has an absolute value for Husserl; he wants thereby to return to absolute being or life, the source of all being.[175]

The thesis of the ontological value inherent to subjectivity and to its intrinsic meaning constitutes the true basis of all Husserl's thought. To be is to be experienced or to have a meaning in life. The phenomenological reduction has no other goal than to present us with our genuine self, although it presents it only to a purely contemplative and theoretical sight which considers life but is distinct from it.

172. *Ibid.*, introduction, p. 1; § 33, p. 57; § 76, p. 142; and especially § 97, p. 204; § 135, pp. 278–79; § 145, pp. 302–3; *Phil. als str. Wiss.*, p. 301 [p. 90].

173. *Ideen*, § 33, p. 57.

174. *Ibid.*, § 135, p. 278; § 147, p. 306.

175. *Ibid.*, § 51, pp. 95–96.

The reduction does not attempt to perform a mere abstraction (our presentation has tried to show this) which imagines consciousness without the world. On the contrary, it discovers our truly concrete life,[176] and it is rather in the psychological attitude in which man is perceived as a part of nature that the meaning of his existence is warped.

However, if this operation seems to be a sort of abstraction, it is a wavering in Husserl's conception of consciousness which is responsible. We have shown that intentionality defines the very nature of consciousness, and we have characterized this intentionality as *necessarily transcendent*. Husserl's texts and the general spirit of his philosophy seem to authorize this; the world seems to be indispensable to a consciousness which is always a consciousness of something. The idea of a transcendent intentionality is so predominant that internal intentionality, that constituted by the hyletic data,[177] is, maybe wrongly, conceived by Husserl to be of the same type. Nevertheless, Husserl does suggest in many texts that he does not think that the idea of pure immanence is contradictory and hence that consciousness could exist without the world. It is probably because of this indecision, or rather because of this obscurity in the relation between *hyle* and *noesis*, that the reduction seems to be a return to a consciousness without the world in which the world would have to be constituted on the basis of a pure *hyle*, a type of abstraction in which one seems to see a revival of the sensationalist theses.

There is another reason why the phenomenological reduction, as we have interpreted it so far, does not reveal concrete life and the meaning that objects have for concrete life. Concrete life is not the solipsist's life of a consciousness closed upon itself. Concrete being is not what exists for only one consciousness. In the very idea of concrete being is contained the idea of an intersubjective world. If we limit ourselves to describing the constitution of objects in an individual consciousness, in an *ego*, we will never reach objects as they are in concrete life but will reach only an abstraction. The reduction to an *ego*, the *egological reduction*, can be only a first step toward phenomenology. We must also discover "others" and the intersubjective world. A phenomenological intuition of the life of others, a reflection by *Einfühlung* opens the field of transcendental intersubjectivity

176. *Ibid.,* p. 95.
177. See above, p. 47.

and completes the work of the philosophical intuition of subjectivity. Here again, the problems of the constitution of the world will arise.[178]

The works of Husserl published so far make only very brief mentions of an intersubjective reduction.[179] We can do no more than repeat what Husserl has said. However, we believe that this intersubjective reduction and all the problems that arise from it have much preoccupied Husserl. He has studied the *Einfühlung*, the intuition through which intersubjectivity becomes accessible; he has described the role played in the *Einfühlung* by the perception of our body and its analogy with the body of others; he has analyzed the life which manifests in this other body a type of existence analogous to mine. Finally, he has examined the characteristic of the constitution proper to intersubjectivity, the conscious reality without which no existence at all would be possible.[180] Although his unpublished works have been very influential, we are not authorized to use them prior to their publication.

178. *Ideen*, § 135, p. 279; § 151, p. 317.
179. *Ibid.*, § 29, pp. 51–52; § 45, p. 84; § 48, p. 90; § 49, p. 92; § 66, pp. 124–25; *Phil. als str. Wiss.*, p. 313 [p. 108].
180. Let us also mention some other problems that are treated in the unpublished works, problems that have no immediate relation to the one with which we are dealing. Some are the existence of man as a person and the history and origin of consciousness (*Ideen*, § 76, p. 142); one can even find a problem such as that of destiny. The investigations of the constitution of immanent time and of cosmic time have assumed an especially great importance. See *Ideen*, §§ 81, 82, pp. 161–65; § 118, pp. 245–46; see also *Zeitbewusstsein*.

Conclusion

LET US again consider briefly the theses we have advanced in the course of this study.

In trying to understand the theory of intuition on the basis of a theory of being, we have tried to show how Husserl goes beyond the naturalistic ontology which hypostatizes the physical objects and conceives the whole of reality on this model. We reached a notion of being which is closely tied to that of "experience." Experience, in turn, has shown itself as absolute being always carrying the guarantee of its own existence, as the locus where all being is constituted, and as essentially intentional.

It follows that conscious life is not faced with its own states but is constantly in the presence of transcendent beings. Under these conditions, truth lies, not in the internal legality of subjective representations, but in the presence of life to its objects given "in person" (*selbstda*). Intuition is the act which claims to put us in contact with being and is the sole *locus* of truth. Once intuition has been so characterized, one can easily understand its extension to the sphere of categories and essences.

The notion of the absolute existence of consciousness—and its primacy with respect to the other regions of reality—allows us to give credence to the claims of intuition. Intuition is an act whose intrinsic meaning consists in giving us objects "in person"; so that the data of intuition need not, in order to be true, be compared with a true being which would be independent of consciousness. The very notions of transcendence and of being are determined through intuition: far from having to be justified by their correspondence to being, the data of intuition are the origin of existence and provide its norms. The theory of intuition rests, therefore, in the last analysis, on the theory of the primacy of consciousness, which claims that all existence is determined by the intrinsic meaning of our life.

It is also by virtue of this primacy of the intrinsic meaning of our life that a new dimension is opened in the investigation of being. One may ask what the specific mode is in which each category of objects is manifested in life. What is the intrinsic meaning of life which is manifested in the constitution of the various regions of objects?

We have tried to show that these questions do not merely concern the structure of life as it reaches these objects, and that they do not pertain merely to the theory of knowledge, but that, by virute of the origin of all being in life, they investigate *the meaning of the very existence of being.*

The deeply philosophical task of this investigation is incumbent on *reflection, which is philosophical intuition.* However, in order to be philosophical, reflection must be directed not toward a psychological consciousness which belongs to the world of transcendent objects, but toward the pure, primary, and eminently concrete consciousness discovered by phenomenological reduction.

We have interpreted the constitutional problems as ontological problems and we have seen their essential task: to throw light on the meaning of existence. This interpretation, which seems to clarify the philosophical role *par excellence* of the phenomenology of consciousness, may be the aspect in which we have been more explicit than Husserl himself. But there is no doubt that he saw this point. "Was besagt dass Gegenständlichkeit sei" is, according to the *Logos* article, the essential problem raised by the phenomenology of consciousness.

Only Heidegger dares to face this problem deliberately, it having been considered impossible by the whole of traditional philosophy. This problem has for its object the meaning of the existence of being, and attempts to find the meaning of Aristotle's "transcendence," the meaning of the "substantiality of substance." We have emphasized one consequence of Husserl's philosophy, the identification of the existence of being with the way being encounters life and the role which it plays in life, a role which becomes visible in the constitution of objects. This is a consequence which seems also to have been noticed by Heidegger and to have influenced him. He appears to follow the way indicated by Husserl on those two points, although in a profoundly original manner, and we feel justified in being inspired by him.

To grasp in an eidetic intuition (the only intuition which reveals necessary relations) all the meanderings of phenomena, we have seen that Husserl elaborates the notion of vague and inexact essences which, under the influences of natural sciences and of naturalism, were considered as purely subjective and without value for the knowledge of being. Husserlian intuition wants to respect the moving and inexact forms of concrete reality. The intellect *qua* faculty of knowing ideal being is not foreign to intuition, and intuition *qua* perception of something that is refractory to mathematization does not contradict the intellect. We have overcome the Bergsonian antagonism between intellect and intuition.

But it is another aspect which shows the deeply intellectualist character of Husserl's intuitionism. Bergson's philosophical intuition tightly bound to man's concrete life and destiny, reaches to its highest point, namely, the act of freedom. This metaphysical foundation of intuition is lacking in Husserl's phenomenology, and the ties which relate intuition to all the vital forces which define concrete existence are foreign to his thought. Philosophy begins with the reduction. This is an act in which we consider life in all its concreteness but no longer live it. Let us examine this point more closely.

Husserl conceives philosophy as a universally valid science in the manner of geometry and the sciences of nature, as a science which is developed through the efforts of generations of scientists, each continuing the work of the others.[1] What is deeply intellectualist in this conception is not that it takes as a model geometry and natural science *qua* sciences of matter which proceed by means of exact concepts. We have seen that Husserl does not borrow from these sciences their rigid type of concept. To take geometry as a model means—and this is what is important—that the function, the role of philosophy, and the role of the sciences in our life, are of the same type; that philosophy occupies the same place in the metaphysical destiny of man as the exercise of the theoretical sciences. *In this conception, philosophy seems as independent of the historical situation of man as any theory that tries to consider everything sub specie aeternitatis.*

1. *See Phil. als str. Wiss.*

Let us say in a few words what we mean by "the historical situation of man." We are not concerned with the fact that the empirical constitution of man is not everywhere and in all the moments of history the same, and that consequently man changes and that the science which is valid at one time may be meaningless at another. Skepticism, which makes use of such arguments derived from a naturalist comprehension of history, is defeated by Husserl's arguments in Volume I of the *Logische Untersuchungen* and, especially, in the second part of "Philosophie als strenge Wissenschaft." Neither naturalistic psychology nor history, being themselves empirical sciences, can shake the certainty of science and its validity *sub specie aeternitatis* which is inherent to the intrinsic meaning of scientific life.[2] The historical situation of man is considered in another sense. It is in life that we must search for the origin of reality, for the origin of the objects of perception as well as of the sciences. This life has a historical character in the sense in which it is said that "all men have a history." It is through this *sui generis* phenomenon in the constitution of a personality that man has a specific manner of being his past that is inconceivable in the case of a stone. Moreover, this historicity is not a secondary property of man as if man existed first and then became temporal and historical. Historicity and temporality form the very substantiality of man's substance.

This structure of consciousness, which occupies a very important place in the thought of someone like Heidegger, for example, could also have a place in the Husserlian framework, inasmuch as it requires only that we respect the intrinsic meaning of the phenomena. Yet, it has not been studied by Husserl, at least in the works published so far. He never discusses the relation between the historicity of consciousness and its intentionality, its personality, its social character.

The absence of this problem in Husserl's works seems to be determined mainly by the general spirit of his thought. The

2. Mr. Shestov has devoted two articles to Husserl in the *Revue philosophique* ("Memento mori," Vol. CI [1926], and "Qu'est-ce que la vérité?" Vol. CIII [1927]), in which he attacks Husserl's intellectualism. He seems, however, to attack one of the strongest points in support of Husserl's intellectualism: its arguments against skeptical and naturalistic psychologism. What we consider Husserl's intellectualism is of a quite different order. From our point of view, skepticism itself need not necessarily be anti-intellectualist.

historicity of consciousness does not appear as an original phenomenon, because the suprahistorical attitude of theory supports, according to Husserl, all our conscious life. The admission of representation as the basis of all acts of consciousness undermines the historicity of consciousness and gives intuition an intellectualist character.

For the same reason, the phenomenological reduction needs no explanation. The reduction is an act by which a philosopher reflects upon himself and, so to speak, "neutralizes" in himself the man living in the world, the man positing the world as existing, the man taking part in the world. The reduction consists in looking at one's life. But by virtue of the primacy of theory, Husserl does not wonder how this "neutralization" of our life,[3] which nevertheless is still an act of our life, has its foundation in life. How does man in the naïve attitude, immersed in the world, the "born dogmatic,"[4] suddenly become aware of his naïveté? Is there here an act of freedom which is metaphysically important for the essence of our life? When Husserl wonders whether the phenomenological reduction can be performed and whether this possibility does not contradict the essence of consciousness,[5] he seems for a moment to be touching on the problem of determining the place of the reduction itself in the life of consciousness. Although he solves this problem by talking of our freedom to neutralize the "existential thesis" of the naïve attitude in order to begin looking at it, the freedom in question here, analogous to doubt, is the freedom of theory. We are led to effectuate the reduction because we can, and because it opens a new field of knowledge. The freedom and the impulse which lead us to reduction and philosophical intuition present by themselves nothing new with respect to the freedom and stimulation of theory. The latter is taken as primary, so that Husserl gives himself the freedom of theory just as he gives himself theory.

Consequently, despite the revolutionary character of the phenomenological reduction, the revolution which it accomplishes is, in Husserl's philosophy, possible only to the extent that the natural attitude is theoretical. The historical role of the reduction and the meaning of its appearance at a certain moment of existence are, for him, not even a problem.

3. *Ideen,* § 110, p. 223.
4. *Ibid.,* § 61, p. 117.
5. *Ibid.,* § 31, p. 53.

The proposition according to which there is a representation at the basis of any act has, therefore, a greater impact on the spirit of Husserl's philosophy, and on the intellectualist character of intuition, than one may believe.

While asserting the primacy of theory for Husserl, we have also emphasized that his essential thesis consists in locating being in concrete life. This is why practical and aesthetic life also have an intentional character and the objects constituted by them also belong to the sphere of being. The aesthetic and ethical categories are also constitutive of being and their mode of existing, and of meeting consciousness have a specific structure. Of course, they are always founded on a purely theoretical experience; the specificity of the being of these "objects of value," etc., is not completely *sui generis* as long as there remains in them something of the brute thing. But isn't the possibility of overcoming this difficulty or fluctuation in Husserl's thought provided with the affirmation of the intentional character of practical and axiological life?

Index